"In this riveting memoir, Bobby Ehnow reveals how it is possible to recover from brokenness with wisdom, virtue, and faith. Because of his rare mixture of personal discipline and unconditional empathy, Bobby has become the nation's behind-the-scenes leader of restorative justice in the Catholic Church."

— **David Karp**, PhD, Professor and Director
of the Center for Restorative Justice
in the Kroc School of Peace Studies
at the University of San Diego

"Deacon Bobby's book *All Things New* takes the reader on a journey from his personal valley in prison back to his mountaintop of faith and love with his family and parish community. *All Things New* brings to life God's justice, perfected with His Son's sacrifice on the cross and continually perfected through mercy and forgiveness."

— **Bishop Michael Pham**
Bishop, Diocese of San Diego

"Deacon Bobby's testimony—from incarceration to a life devoted to full ministry to the incarcerated—is undoubtedly a journey from brokenness to restoration. With candor and conviction, he shows how his own wounds have become a source of healing and hope for those he serves in his ministry, including individuals who are currently or formerly incarcerated and their families. Bobby's story will resonate with anyone who believes in second chances and the power of redemption."

— **Bishop Ramon Bejarano**
Bishop, Diocese of Monterey

"I first knew Bobby as one of my doctoral students, before he went to prison. I have come to know him since as one of my spiritual teachers. This book traces his costly passage—from commanding officer of Marines to businessman, through the crucible of imprisonment, to compassionate servant—one who now speaks confidently to politicians, judges, bishops and cardinals, and with humility to the wounded and forgotten."

— **Sister Terri Monroe**, RSCJ, Ed. D.
Retired Associate Professor, Leadership Studies,
University of San Diego

"Deacon Bobby Ehnow has lived an inspiring story. Yet it is not a new story. It is the story of Saint Peter and Saint Paul, Saint Augustine and Saint Francis. It is also our story. It is the story of redemption; a real-life narrative proclaiming this truth: there is hope for everyone."

— **Father Mike Murphy**
Pastor, Sacred Heart Catholic Church, Coronado

"*All Things New* is a testament to the capacity for transformation in all of us and the power of God's redeeming Grace. Dr. Ehnow boldly invites readers to share in his journey of restoration alongside his family, Scripture, the communion of saints, and his incarcerated brothers and sisters."

— **Caitlin Morneau**,
Director of Restorative Justice,
Catholic Mobilizing Network

ALL THINGS NEW

Living the Feminist Dream
A Faithful Vision for Women in the Church and the World
by Kate Bryan

Keep at it, Riley!
Accompanying my Father through Death into Life
by Noreen Madden McInnes

Rehumanize
A Vision to Secure Human Rights for All
by Aimee Murphy

The Church's Mission in a Polarized World
by Aaron Wessman

The Perils of Perfection
On the Limits and Possibilities of Human Enhancement
by Joseph Vukov

Staying Human
In an Era of Artificial Intelligence
by Joseph Vukov

ALL THINGS NEW

A Journey from Brokenness to Restoration

Bobby Ehnow

NEW CITY PRESS

Published in the United States by New City Press
136 Madison Avenue, Floors 5 & 6, PMB #4290
New York, NY 10016
www.newcitypress.com

All Things New
A Journey from Brokenness to Restoration

Cover and Layout by Miguel Tejerina

ISBN: 978-1-56548-742-0 (Paperback)
ISBN: 978-1-56548-743-7 (E-book)

Library of Congress Control Number: 2026936192

Printed in the United States of America

Contents

Series Preface

Does the book that you are about to read seem unusual? Perhaps even counterintuitive?

Good. The Magenta series wouldn't be doing its job if you felt otherwise.

On the color wheel, magenta lies directly between red and blue. Just so, books in this series do not lie at one limit or another of our hopelessly simplistic, two-dimensional, antagonistic, binary imagination. Often, in the broader culture any answer to a moral or political question gets labeled as liberal or conservative, red or blue. But the Magenta series refuses to play by these shortsighted rules. Magenta will address the complexity of the issues of our day by resisting a framework that unnecessarily pits one idea against another. Magenta refuses to be defined by anything other than a positive vision of the good.

If you understand anything about the Focolare's dialogical-and-faithful mission, it should not surprise you that this series has found a home with the Focolare's New City Press. The ideas in these books, we believe, will spark dialogues that will heal divides and build unity at the very sites of greatest fragmentation and division.

The ideas in Magenta are crucial not only for our fragmented culture, but also for the Church. Our secular idolatry—our simplistic left/right, red/blue imagination—has oozed into the Church as well, disfiguring the Body of Christ with ugly disunity. Such idolatry, it must be said, has muffled the Gospel and crippled the Church, keeping it from being salt and light in a wounded world desperate for unity.

Magenta is not naïve. We realize full well that appealing to dialogue or common ground can be dismissed as a weak-sauce, milquetoast attempt to cloud our vision of the good or reduce it to a mere least common denominator. We know that much dialogic spade work is yet to be done, but that does not keep the vision of the Magenta Series (like the color it bears) from being *bold*. There is nothing half-hearted about it. All our authors have a brilliant, attractive vision of the good.

Welcoming this new book from "Bobby," as many of us call him, is one of the true highlights of the series. It is difficult to imagine a more appropriate book, a more appropriate story, outlining the vision of human dignity Magenta attempts to articulate and promote into our polarized world. In offering us his own story, Bobby gives us a front-row seat—not only to how God's justice is perfected through mercy, love, and forgiveness—but also to how US American justice is currently based on values that are inconsistent with our values as a Church.

Here's something extremely hopeful: criminal justice reform is one of the few areas where there are real possibilities for bi-partisan reform in ways which bypass our deep problems of polarization. For example, at the federal level, we've seen the Second Chance Act (2008) and First Step Act (2018) passed and celebrated by a range of people who in other contexts are deeply opposed on many issues. There is also bipartisan support in several states and localities for similar steps to be taken.

But before we move too quickly to political strategy and public policy, I urge us to take full stock of Bobby's story. To let it in. Let it shape our minds and hearts. And then prayerfully ask for direction in moving us to action.

Enjoy!

Charles C. Camosy
Series Editor

Foreword

By Paul Callan

"Here begins the descent.
Here begin the terrors and the miracles.
Here begins the quest."
—Perlesvaus

I have always been attracted to epic stories like the Arthurian Legends, The Grail Quest, the trials of Prometheus and Theseus, and Homer's Odyssey. I am drawn to the symbolism and allegory used to convey deeper meanings and universal truths, as well as the archetypal characters like the hero, the mentor, and the trickster, who together animate these journey themes. Most specifically, I am captivated by the series of tests the heroes must overcome to achieve their goals, which usually involve a deep inner conversion to make them worthy of the boon they pursue. Though enchanted by these tales, I never imagined I would come to know someone who lived through such ordeals and be similarly transformed by them.

Enter Bobby Ehnow.

I first met Bobby thirty years ago when, as young Marine Corps Officers, we were both stationed at Headquarters, U.S. Marine Corps, in Washington, DC. In the following decades we formed a deep friendship and professional rapport through our devotion to the Corps, and most recently, in our service to the Catholic Diocese of San Diego. Although I thought very highly of Bobby as a Marine, my admiration for him has grown exponentially after he endured his dark night of the soul while incarcerated. His progression through the prison system, and his ordeal as a prisoner, reveals the same down-then-up trajectory one would also recognize in the transformations of Parzival, King Arthur, and Odysseus. While imprisoned, Bobby underwent a changed consciousness where he no longer wrote his story; now his story was being written through him.

In the chapters that follow, Bobby courageously discloses his highs and lows, victories and defeats, and joys and pains. As other commentators have well noted, absolute victory or total defeat do not always corrupt, sometimes they reveal. For it is our response to victory and defeat that uncovers our true character in equal measure. The highs are heady stuff. The lows hurt a lot. But in retrospect, the lessons gleaned from loss clarify and guide us more truthfully than any temporary joy we savor in victory. Our losses, compared to the wisdom gained through life's crucible, would barely fill a thimble cup.

Bobby's memoir reminds us that to transform ourselves we must first go inside the labyrinth's center to learn the right questions. The Franciscan Richard Rohr notes that, in classic lore, this labyrinthine quest was a common developmental theme, where Achilles wore a breastplate adorned with a labyrinth in his conquest of Troy and Theseus slayed the Minotaur only by navigating the maze via Ariadne's felicitous thread. Within each person, hubris must confront nemesis. And by faithfully navigating his maze, Bobby discovered this ennobling insight: You are not what happened to you; you are ultimately what you make of yourself by accepting God's love and mercy.

Bobby's example is a timely warning to the rest of us, to avoid the pitfall of believing life is mostly upward and smooth. Truth is, human flourishing is always menaced by entropy. Jacob did not become fully manifest without wrestling the Angel and acquiring a limp. We learn more from failure than from success, and suffering, though painful in the moment, is still the most direct path to truth. Moreover, Bobby shows us that character development is most firmly crystallized at the crossroads and in the margins, when we are stuck between Scylla and Charybdis, and it is only through the scalding rinse of internal spiritual struggle that conversion happens. Wise commentators like Richard Rohr have said in words what Bobby's life reveals in experience: transformation is not something we do; it is something being done to us.

Bobby's journey also reveals we are all capable of two types of character in life: character of the ascent and character of the descent. Character of the ascent is the persona of the public square; our accomplishments, titles, and bona fides. The ascent is generally the first phase of our life when we see the ladder before us and we willingly climb it. The character of the ascent places us, the climber, at the center of all dramas. As the author David Brooks noted, this is the time of resume virtues. Some people reach this stage and remain there, even into old age, and thus engage life solely from this narrow self-centered mindset.

Others accept the necessity of the ascent, because it served a formative purpose, but they also understand it is now limiting, so they turn and head back down. Here begins forging the character of the descent, which is a time where humility and magnanimity slowly emerge, brought on by necessary defeats and the empty calories of hubris. Ego cracks, individual success seems less relevant, and we look to serve others. Only now are we prepared to form what Brooks called eulogy virtues.

And paradoxically, as Maria Popova of *The Marginalian* said, in letting go we finally find the things worth holding on to. Much of our ultimate happiness rises from the ruin of our best laid plans, when we learn to harness the catalytic power of suffering. This is the stage of life where one is truly imperfect yet complete. Further drawing from Popova's insights into spiritual conversion, we can understand how the polytropos quality of Bobby's journey, his ups and downs and twists and turns, made who he is today, and how his joys and defeats became sacred adornments of his character. His crucible healed him, allowing loss to form the full tapestry of his life. And via life's natural winnowing process, Bobby finally discovered that obedience, genuflection, and willingness are strengths, not weaknesses.

Bobby Ehnow followed the descent and emerged not just changed, but better, because he recognized the blessed character of his joys and sufferings and resolved to be true to them. No bland theory here, only human goodness fully tested by life and a soul now profoundly transformed and amplified on the road to a generative life.

Part I

Inside

"The worst prison would be a closed heart."
—St. John Paul II

Chapter 1

We Are All God's Children

Introduction

As the first decade of the twenty-first century came to a close, I believed I was at the pinnacle of success. After a rewarding twenty-year career, in 2008 I retired from the U.S. Marine Corps. Shortly afterward, I purchased an industrial tool and supply company with several Department of Defense contracts. Under my leadership, in under two years the company's revenue tripled—from just over one million dollars annually to more than three million. I was earning more than I had ever imagined. My wife, Colette, had also recently transitioned from active duty as a Navy ophthalmologist to private practice with the Southern California Permanente Medical Group. If success was measured in money, then Colette and I were thriving—firmly in the top 1 percent of earners.

Colette and I met in 2003 while we were both serving in the military. After a year of dating, we married and blended our families—my two children and her two very young children. Merging two families presented challenges, but we felt blessed as we built our new life together. Early in our marriage, that life was tested when my Marine Corps unit was deployed. As the commanding officer, I spent thirteen months in Iraq—absent from my new bride and family throughout 2006 and into 2007. When my unit returned to the U.S., Colette and I decided to leave military service to focus on our family. She had served twelve years on active duty, plus four years at the Uniformed Services University of Health Sciences. I had completed twenty years and was eligible to retire as a lieutenant colonel. Though we loved serving our country and leading Marines and Sailors, we chose to prioritize raising our children.

We believed we were living the American Dream. We owned a home in a beautiful coastal community in San Diego, a second home near Park City, Utah, and a recreational vehicle to travel between them. We also owned a rental property in downtown San Diego and had more disposable income than we knew what to do with. We were active in our church, tried to be generous with our resources, and were well regarded in our community. Life felt incredibly good. I had a loving family, a beautiful and intelligent wife, and more money than one could reasonably need. But that seemingly idyllic life was about to unravel.

On January 20, 2011, around 6:30 a.m., twelve federal agents from the FBI, IRS Criminal Investigations Division, Naval Criminal Investigative Service (NCIS), and Defense Criminal Investigative Service (DCIS) knocked on my front door. I was served a federal search warrant for my home and informed I was the target of a criminal investigation for wire fraud, money laundering, bribery, major government fraud, and tax evasion. At the same time, thirteen agents from those same agencies served a warrant at my business. The phrase "shock and awe" perfectly describes that day—a day I thought would be routine. Instead, it marked the beginning of nearly a decade of legal battles, both criminal and civil, for me, my business, and my family.

This book is not an autobiography, though many parts of my life story are included. It focuses on my experiences with the criminal and civil justice systems—both as a defendant and as someone who has ministered to others navigating those systems. This is the story of a fall from the heights of worldly success to the depths of personal failure. But more importantly, it's about the internal transformation that followed—a journey from pride and self-importance to humility and mercy. It's about the mistakes I made through poor decisions, and the grace I received through the unwavering love of my family, friends, and community.

I am grateful to have been knocked down and brought low. I've learned that life's most meaningful lessons often come not through victory, but failure. Most importantly, I've come to believe that each of us is called to love one another—with tolerance, forgiveness, and mercy. In telling this story I hope to provide a clear and honest view of the American criminal justice system—particularly its corrections model—and how it often fails both those who have been harmed and those who have caused harm. I pray that as you read, your heart will be moved toward mercy and forgiveness for those who have stumbled, made poor choices, or committed crimes—and now find themselves behind bars.

CONAIR

In early June 2013, I boarded a specially designed Boeing 737 operated by the Justice Prisoner and Alien Transportation System (JPATS), more commonly known as CONAIR. I was a prisoner being transported from the Federal Transfer Center in Oklahoma City to the Federal Prison Complex in Florence, Colorado.

On CONAIR, inmates are typically shackled together in pairs. For this leg of the journey, I was shackled to a foreign-born inmate known to the outside world as Ramzi Yousef—one of the principal architects of the 1993 World

Trade Center bombing, a committed Islamic terrorist, and the nephew of Khalid Sheikh Mohammed (KSM), the mastermind of the 9/11 attacks. Ramzi Yousef used an alias; he introduced himself to me simply as Mahmoud.

By divine providence, for most of that day, a retired U.S. Marine Corps Lieutenant Colonel—me—sat, waited, and spoke with one of the most notorious terrorists held in U.S. custody. I, a practicing Catholic and a Marine, had spent twenty years in uniform, including four combat tours in the Middle East during the Global War on Terrorism. Nearly half of my military career involved preparing for or executing deployments to confront men like Ramzi—those committed to harming Americans and attacking our ideals. As a logistics officer and commander, my job was to support Marine aviation units engaged in combat operations against individuals just like him.

Mahmoud, by contrast, was a devout Muslim and, by his own admission, a cold-blooded killer. In our opening exchange, he told me of the first person he ever killed, a Jew in the West Bank. Not to be intimidated, I replied, "I've never killed a Jew or a Christian, but in my professional life, my organization has killed thousands of Muslims." In prison, you learn quickly that intimidation must be met with resolve—and sometimes I escalated when I probably shouldn't have. But after that initial exchange of bravado, something surprising happened: we had a meaningful conversation about Judaism, Christianity, and Islam. I was shocked to discover that Mahmoud knew more scripture than I did—and I'm a cradle Catholic. Perhaps not that surprising after all.

We spent about seven hours together. Our lives couldn't have been more different. I grew up in a middle-class suburb outside Philadelphia, raised Catholic by loving parents who taught my brother and me the values of faith, family, discipline, and respect for all life—including for those less fortunate than us. My childhood revolved around Catholic school, church, sports, and family activities. We were the embodiment of the Leave It to Beaver generation—raised by Bud and Betty Ehnow, known in our neighborhood as the Cleavers of Pennsylvania.

My upbringing led me to Villanova University and then to the Marine Corps. For the first four decades of my life, I was shaped by two of the largest institutions in the world: the Roman Catholic Church and the U.S. government. I had every advantage—a stable home, a strong education, and a clear path toward personal and professional success. Yet despite that foundation, poor judgment and unchecked ambition led me to that fateful day, shackled to Mahmoud on a prison transport plane.

Mahmoud was born in Kuwait and raised in Pakistan. Like me, he had received a university education. But unlike me, his path led to radicalization and terrorism. In one sense, we were alike: two educated men who wanted to make a difference in the world. But our worldviews couldn't have been further apart. Mine was rooted in love, justice, and service. His was grounded in ideological hatred for Western ideals, with violence as a justified means to an end. In the short time we spent together, I learned little about what radicalized him—but I was struck by how much we were able to exchange simply because we were both prisoners.

My life led me to serve and defend my nation; his life led him to wage war against it. I sacrificed for a cause I believed was just. Mahmoud believed his cause was equally righteous. I have friends who admire my choice to serve; I'm certain he has family and friends who view his actions with similar admiration—however misguided that may be.

Despite our differences, we had two undeniable things in common that day. First, we were both convicted criminals. We wore the same disposable prison clothes, were identified by numbers instead of names, and were under the constant supervision of federal correctional officers. Mahmoud was returning to ADMAX Florence to serve the remainder of his 240-year sentence in solitary confinement—twenty-three hours a day with no human contact. For him, a trip to New York (likely as a witness in a terrorism case) was a rare break in an otherwise monotonous existence. His earthly life will end in isolation, in one of the most secure prisons in the world—home at the time to infamous inmates like Ted Kaczynski, Terry Nichols, and Michael Swango.

I, on the other hand, was headed to the Federal Prison Camp at Florence—a facility designed for non-violent offenders, including many convicted of white-collar crimes or drug offenses. After being found guilty at trial I had been sentenced to thirty-six months. Prior to that, I spent four months at the San Diego Metropolitan Correctional Center awaiting sentencing. Florence would be my home for twenty-three months, until I was released to a halfway house and eventually home confinement in May 2015. After that day with Mahmoud, I never saw or heard from him again. He returned to invisibility—his only human interaction with the guards who moved him to a cage for brief periods of exercise a few times a week.

As I reflect now, our second shared reality has become even more significant: we were both created in the image and likeness of God. Though Mahmoud's crimes were unspeakably evil, God loves him as much as he loves me—and as much as he loves you. That truth may be hard to accept, but I believe it with all my heart.

In Prison

I consider it a blessing that I went to prison—and an even greater blessing that my sentence was relatively short.

Before my incarceration, I lived like a modern-day Pharisee, convinced I was one of the "good guys," believing that some people simply didn't deserve the dignity that God guarantees to each of his children. But prison is a great equalizer. There, a retired Marine officer and a notorious terrorist share the same lowly status. In prison I began to understand what God did for us when he became one of us. My descent—from a life of prestige and entitlement to the depths of incarceration—was the result of my pride and poor judgment, but it became the beginning of true transformation.

That experience opened my eyes to a central tenet of Catholic Social Teaching: the inherent dignity of every person. Each of us is a moral agent. As Christians, we believe that every human being deserves dignity simply by virtue of being one of God's creations. We also believe in justice, mercy, and forgiveness. Accountability is necessary. I committed a crime and deserved to be held responsible. I was fortunate to receive a just sentence—firm but not excessive. Similarly, Mahmoud was responsible for the deaths of seven people, including one unborn child, in the 1993 World Trade Center bombing. He deserves to spend the rest of his life in prison.

Still, for those of us who believe in the dignity of all human life, the real challenge is reconciling justice with love—especially for those who have caused great harm. My faith demands that I accept a difficult truth: the unborn child who died in a terrorist attack and the terrorist who caused that death both possess equal human dignity. That notion contradicts reason and certainly contradicts modern justice, yet it is central to the Gospel. Mahmoud's actions were undeniably evil, and yet Jesus commands us to "love our neighbor." That doesn't mean Mahmoud should go free—he deserves a life sentence—but even so, he remains one of God's creations.

In prison, I met many people who had done terrible things. And yet, I also discovered my own capacity to love men who, by the world's standards, didn't deserve it. I found that many of them struggled to love themselves—a critical barrier to healing and forgiveness.

When I was first incarcerated, I didn't believe I belonged in prison. I thought my crimes weren't serious enough to warrant such punishment. I had been remanded immediately after my guilty verdict, and my first four months were spent in the San Diego Metropolitan Correctional Center (MCC)—a federal detention facility where inmates await trial or sentencing. It was my first exposure to a world marked by violence, despair, and, in many cases, injustice.

Due to a chronic condition that required daily medication and consistent medical access I was assigned to the eleventh floor. Soon after I arrived one of the correctional officers, a former Marine, pulled me aside. He explained that the eleventh-floor housed inmates with medical and psychological conditions, sexual offenders, and those in protective custody. He warned me to be cautious. Despite my attempts to keep a low profile, nearly every inmate already seemed to know who I was and what I had done.

My first two cellmates helped me adjust to life inside. Patrick was a drug dealer from Northern California who had been growing large quantities of marijuana. He had taken a plea deal and expected a twenty-four-month sentence. Patrick was friendly and open about his Christian faith. He believed that getting caught was a blessing—an opportunity to change his life. Sadly, we only lived together for two weeks. One day, while watching TV in the common area, in a racially motivated conflict, Patrick was stabbed in the jugular. I was in our cell and didn't witness the attack. I later learned he survived and had been transferred to a different prison. I still think of Patrick often and pray for him.

My other cellmate, Mark, had been a homeless, lifelong drug addict. He referred to himself as being on the "life installment plan," meaning he had spent most of his adult life cycling in and out of prison. Though half Filipino, Mark identified as Caucasian and had a swastika tattoo from his time in the Aryan Brotherhood in state prison. The fact that he had once shared a cell with an African American man like Patrick, and then lived with me, was only possible because the eleventh floor was supposedly free of "prison politics."

For most of my four months at the MCC Mark and I lived together. He was serving time for a probation violation after testing positive for drugs. He chose incarceration over the burden of regular drug testing. He frequently used heroin in our cell, which made me extremely nervous—any drugs found there would have implicated me, too. Despite that, we spent many long nights talking about life, family, and love. Mark wanted to change, but after decades of addiction and crime, didn't know how. He was already sixty years old. I still think of him and pray that he found his way out of addiction.

After Patrick's departure, our new cellmate was Luis, a Mexican national with a long criminal history. He had been caught crossing the U.S.-Mexico border with outstanding warrants. His children lived legally in the U.S., and he crossed illegally to see them. Luis said he couldn't be deported because he was wanted by a cartel in Mexico. Like me, he was Catholic, and we attended Mass together on Saturday evenings in the MCC chapel. Luis was a good man with many struggles—addiction, homelessness, mental illness—all of which contributed to his criminal behavior. I lived with Mark and Luis for the remainder of my time at the MCC.

Most inmates I met did not have the educational background I had. I was a product of Catholic schools from first grade through college. By the time I was incarcerated, I had two master's degrees and was working on a doctorate. That level of education was rare in the prison system. Early on, I met a former MS-13 gang member, Miguel, a young man from El Salvador. I knew he was affiliated because "MS-13" was tattooed across his face and body.

Miguel had dropped out of school in fifth grade and later defected from MS-13. That's why he was on the eleventh floor. If he had been housed with the general population, he would've been a target. You don't simply walk away from a gang like MS-13. Miguel asked for help drafting legal documents related to his case. Many undocumented inmates face deportation after their sentences, and Miguel knew returning to El Salvador would mean death.

We made a deal: I would help him with his legal filings if he prayed the rosary with me each day for two weeks. He agreed, and we honored the deal. Miguel had been raised Catholic, and our prayer time was powerful. It marked the beginning of a nightly habit—I prayed the rosary every evening for the entire 807 days of my incarceration. Miguel was transferred before I left the MCC, and I don't know what became of him. He was born into extreme poverty and trapped in one of the world's most violent gangs. Meeting and praying with him was a profound spiritual gift—something that would never have happened if not for my own mistakes.

My neighbor in the next cell, Dominick, was a self-proclaimed member of the Gambino crime family. I doubted that claim, but we shared a common East Coast background—he was from Brooklyn, I was from Philadelphia—and we bonded over our accents and mutual love of sports. Dominick had spent most of his life in and out of prison. He had come to San Diego for a fresh start but quickly returned to crime. I'm fairly certain he was responsible for smuggling the heroin that Mark used in our cell.

Dominick would often stand on the upper level of our pod and chat with me about sports and life. He loved hearing stories about my Marine Corps service. Every so often, he'd randomly exclaim, "Fuhgeddaboudit," like a character out of a mob movie. He told me he once pulled a lit cigar from Robert De Niro's mouth in his Brooklyn restaurant after the actor refused to stop smoking. "You may play a wise guy in the movies," he said, "but I am one." I never knew whether his stories were true, but I enjoyed his company.

Dominick had children he rarely saw, due to his long stints in prison. As we talked about fatherhood, I realized we had more in common than just our accents. His criminal lifestyle made him an absentee dad; my deployments and career had done the same to me at times. Though I doubted his mob affiliation, I had no doubt he was a career criminal. I'm not sure why he was on the eleventh floor, but there he was.

There were a few other former Marines on our floor. One was Stuart, a young gay man awaiting sentencing for sexual misconduct with a seventeen-year-old boy. He had to be housed in protective custody for his own safety. In prison, sexual offenders, especially those who harm minors —are targeted. Once Dominick learned of Stuart's charges, he threatened him, forcing Stuart to request a move to administrative segregation, or the SHU (Special Housing Unit). As a result, Dominick and a few others were moved to the twelfth floor, the most violent and dangerous unit. I never saw him again.

On the twelfth floor, just one floor from my cell, one of the most notorious criminals in the world awaited sentencing: Eduardo Félix Arellano, the leader of the Tijuana Cartel. He and I shared the same sentencing judge: U.S. District Judge Larry Burns.

Ironically, despite our vastly different crimes, Félix and I were facing similar sentences. He was looking at ten to twenty years; I was facing eleven and a half to thirteen years based on my position as CEO, the dollar amount involved, and the fact that I went to trial instead of accepting a plea deal. Prosecutors recommended a sentence of 134 months—over eleven years. Félix ultimately received fifteen years. I was sentenced to three.

Judge Burns, appointed by President George W. Bush in 2003, had a reputation for being tough but fair. Inmates called him "Burn 'em Burns" for his lengthy sentences. On sentencing day in May 2013 my family and I prepared for the worst. But I had an army of prayer warriors in my corner—parishioners, friends, and family. In a moment of grace, Judge Burns became my first encounter with restorative justice. He reduced my sentence by more than 70 percent, sentencing me to just thirty-six months.

I'll never forget returning to the MCC that evening. Mark and Dominick congratulated me—though I suspect they thought I had cooperated with the government, since such sentence reductions are rare. But I know what happened: a miracle occurred on May 20, 2013, on the fourteenth floor of the San Diego federal courthouse.

God's Children

This book is about mercy, forgiveness, accountability, and—most of all—love. During my first four months in prison, awaiting transfer to Florence, Colorado, I met a cast of characters I never would have encountered in my previous life. My arrogance and poor judgment brought me there, but I'm grateful that I did meet these men. Early in my incarceration, I met Patrick, Luis, Mark, Dominick, Stuart, and Mahmoud—men considered outcasts by society.

For many, it's uncomfortable to suggest that these men deserve the same dignity and respect as an unborn child, a physician, a bank president, or a train conductor. Yet what Jesus teaches is counterintuitive to our modern world: we are called to love all our brothers and sisters. In fact, in the Catholic faith visiting the imprisoned is considered one of the corporal works of mercy—something Christ commands us to do.

Since 2018, I've served the Diocese of San Diego, first as associate director for its jail and prison ministry, and now as director of the Office for Life, Peace, and Justice. I never imagined that my time behind bars was part of God's plan to prepare me for ministry, but it was. God truly has a sense of humor, and his plan is always better than ours. The work I now do on behalf of the Church is a tremendous blessing for me and my family.

The stories in the following chapters are drawn from my personal experience and from those I've served through this ministry. They testify to the living presence of God—Father, Son, and Holy Spirit—within jails and prisons. In those often-forgotten places, God is not absent. He is alive and, in many cases, flourishing.

We are all God's children, loved in ways we can't fully comprehend. Ramzi Yousef, the terrorist I accompanied back to the supermax prison in Florence, will die behind bars. He is a real and ongoing threat to public safety. His crimes and ideology still represent danger. He is, without question, an enemy of the American people.

And yet, I do not believe our encounter was a coincidence. Over a decade ago, Ramzi and I met and broke bread together—well, we shared bologna sandwiches. If I harbored any prejudice in my life, it was against Muslims. It was easy to dislike an entire group of people when fighting a war in a Muslim country. But on that day in June 2013, Ramzi and

I were equals: prisoners and children of God. I continue to pray for him. I pray that his heart has softened.

For those of us who profess to follow Christ, the greatest challenge is to love our enemies. In Matthew's Gospel, Jesus teaches:

> You have heard that it was said, "You shall love your neighbor and hate your enemy. But I say to you, love your enemies, and pray for those who persecute you, so that you may be children of your Father in heaven, for he makes his sun rise on the bad and on the good, and sends rain on the righteous and the unrighteous. For if you love those who love you, what reward do will you have? Be perfect, therefore, just as your heavenly Father is perfect." (5:43–45, 48)

Many saints of the Catholic Church were incarcerated for the "crime" of believing in Jesus. They are remembered for leading heroic, virtuous, and holy lives—even to the point of death. In the next chapter, I'll share stories of these saints, whose courage and faith through adversity inspired me during my own time behind bars.

Chapter 2

The Condemned Prisoner with Jesus

Mercy for the Condemned

God loves us so deeply that he sent his only Son to live among us, teach us, die for us, and rise again in a glorified body three days after his death. This is the foundation of the Christian faith. We believe that Jesus of Nazareth is the Christ, the Son of God, who became man out of love for all humanity. He was the son of Mary and Joseph, a Jew, a carpenter, a teacher, and a first-century religious leader in Palestine. He was also a condemned prisoner, executed on a wooden cross as a criminal—considered a blasphemer by Jewish authorities and a threat by Roman rulers. This image of Jesus as a criminal is not the image we typically associate with the Son of God.

According to the gospels, Jesus was crucified after the Jewish Passover and was resurrected three days later. The risen Jesus appeared to the Apostles and other followers for forty days before ascending to heaven. Interestingly, the gospels do not describe anyone else—apostles, religious leaders, family, or friends of Jesus—being explicitly welcomed into heaven. That doesn't mean they weren't; it's simply not mentioned. But there is one person Jesus unmistakably promises eternal life: a condemned criminal crucified beside him.

Luke's Gospel recounts:

> When they came to the place called the Skull, they crucified him and the criminals there, one on his right, the other on his left. Then Jesus said, "Father, forgive them, they know not what they are doing." They divided his garments by casting lots. The people stood by and watched; the rulers, meanwhile, sneered at him and said, "He saved others, let him save himself if he is the chosen one, the Messiah of God." Even the soldiers jeered at him. As they approached to offer him wine, they called out, "If you are King of the Jews, save yourself." Above him there was an inscription that read, "This is the King of the Jews." Now one of the criminals hanging there reviled Jesus, saying, "Are you not the Messiah? Save yourself and us." The other, however, rebuked him, saying in reply, "Have you no fear of God, for you are subject to the same condemnation? And indeed, we have been condemned justly, for the sentence we received corresponds to our crimes, but this man has done nothing criminal." Then he said, "Jesus, remember me when you come into your kingdom." He replied, "Amen, I say to you, today you will be with me in Paradise." (23:33-43)

Think of all the people Jesus encountered during his public ministry, yet he never singled out anyone else with the promise of heaven. As he was dying, the two men suffering beside him were both criminals, likely guilty of serious offenses. One of them, who expressed faith in Jesus, was shown mercy and given a place in heaven. The Church venerates this man as St. Dismas, the patron saint of prisoners.

Jesus, in his final moments, extended mercy to someone society had written off—an outcast, a criminal, a man who had not lived a holy life. Even as he faced death, Jesus showed compassion. St. Dismas' execution may have satisfied the justice of the ancient world, but Jesus' mercy granted him eternal life.

As someone who broke the law and was incarcerated, I carry the lifelong label "convicted felon," a label shared by nearly twenty million Americans. It carries stigma and shame, not just for the crime, but for what the title implies. Yet Jesus' final act of love on the cross was for a criminal. He didn't focus on what St. Dismas had done; he offered him salvation out of love. St. Dismas didn't earn heaven. Jesus gave it freely. Jesus provided a perfect example of mercy and forgiveness.

I used to recoil at being labeled a criminal. In prison, many referred to themselves as such without hesitation. But the title "criminal" carries a permanence that other labels do not. For instance, those once labeled "homeless" lose that label once they find shelter. But a felony conviction follows you for life.

Today, while I am not proud of my criminal behavior, I find deep comfort in knowing that a fellow convicted criminal was welcomed into heaven because of faith and Jesus' mercy. St. Dismas' story is the perfect example of grace, forgiveness, and redemption. Jesus wasn't concerned about his label, and he isn't concerned about ours.

Mercy Today and Everyday

At Florence Prison Camp, where I was incarcerated, I met an inmate named Sal. He was in his early sixties and fairly active when I first got to know him. We would often see each other exercising at the weight pile or out on the track. About a year later, Sal stopped exercising, and I learned he was seriously ill. Despite obvious physical decline, the prison medical staff accused him of faking. They sent him to a local hospital for evaluation, but no diagnosis was made, and he was returned without further treatment.

Over the next six months, Sal lost more than half his body weight. He became incontinent, wheelchair-bound, and completely dependent on his cellmate, who courageously cared for him. Despite his visible deterioration, the Bureau of Prisons failed to provide proper medical care. After Sal died, an autopsy revealed an undiagnosed brain tumor. His death—preventable and undignified—was a moral failure of the system. No person, regardless of their crimes, should be denied medical care or basic dignity. A just society does not punish with neglect.

Sal was a convicted criminal, but I believe Jesus showed him the same mercy he showed St. Dismas two thousand years ago. Sal's punishment was incarceration, not the denial of humane treatment. Catholic Social Teaching affirms the dignity of every human life. Yet many people struggle to believe that someone who committed a crime deserves the same dignity as someone who has not. This is the great challenge of our faith: to see Christ in every person, especially the imprisoned. I believe Jesus did not judge Sal unworthy of his love. He welcomed him into eternal life. Christians are called to imitate Christ—to love and show mercy, including to those behind bars.

When Jesus told St. Dismas that he would be with him in paradise, he comforted a dying man. But he also offered a message to all of us: we matter, we are loved, and his mercy is available, regardless of our past. St. Dismas believed, and Jesus responded with love.

My spiritual director, Sister Terri Monroe, RSCJ, often refers to the saints as "great allies" in our faith. Saints are models for us as we pursue our own journey of holiness. In my office at the Diocese of San Diego's pastoral center, I have canvas prints of saints and historical figures who give me hope. All of them spent time in jail or prison.

Two of the Church's best-known saints—St. Peter and St. Paul—were imprisoned for proclaiming the gospel. St. Peter was jailed in Jerusalem and imprisoned again in Rome before being martyred by crucifixion. He was the leader of the apostles, yet he, too, was a prisoner—just like Jesus and St. Dismas.

St. Paul encountered the risen Jesus on the road to Damascus and went on to spread the gospel across the Roman Empire. His imprisonments are well documented in both the Acts of the Apostles and his letters. He was arrested in Philippi (and miraculously freed), detained in Jerusalem, and finally placed under house arrest in Rome, where he was eventually martyred. He probably wrote some of his epistles while incarcerated. His "crime" was believing in and preaching about Jesus.

As Catholics, we are blessed to have multiple patron saints for a given cause. St. Dismas is the patron saint of prisoners—an obvious choice, given that he died beside Jesus on the cross. Another is St. Maximilian Kolbe, a widely known twentieth-century martyr. A Polish Franciscan priest, he was murdered by the Nazis at Auschwitz in 1941. Unlike Dismas, Kolbe garners more immediate sympathy. His crime was resisting evil and offering his life in place of another prisoner's. Yet both saints powerfully reveal the mercy of God.

Maximilian Kolbe was born in the Kingdom of Poland when it was under Russian rule. As a child, he had a vision of the Virgin Mary, which shaped his devotion and led him to the priesthood. Ordained in 1918, he earned doctorates in philosophy and theology and later ran a Catholic publishing house focused on Marian devotion. In the 1930s, he served as a missionary in China, Japan, and India.

When Germany invaded Poland in 1939, Father Kolbe had returned home. He turned his monastery into a hospital and was arrested by the gestapo that September but released shortly after. In February 1941, he was arrested again and in May sent to Auschwitz. There, he endured beatings and torture. That July, a prisoner escaped. As punishment, the deputy camp commander chose ten men to die by starvation. When one of the selected men, Franciszek Gajowniczek, cried out for his wife and children, Father Kolbe volunteered to take his place. In the starvation bunker, he led prayers, strengthening the other men. After two weeks, only four prisoners, including Father Kolbe, remained alive, so the Nazis executed them by injecting carbolic acid into their veins. Witnesses reported that Kolbe peacefully raised his arm in surrender. He died a martyr for his faith.

At Auschwitz, survival was rare. Of the 1.3 million prisoners held there, fewer than two hundred thousand lived through the ordeal. Remarkably, Franciszek Gajowniczek survived, was reunited with his family, and lived to the age of ninety-three. He dedicated his life to telling Father Kolbe's story. In 1982, when Saint John Paul II canonized Maximilian Kolbe, Franciszek and his family were present. Kolbe's life and death inspired countless others. In a place utterly devoid of mercy, he embodied mercy and sacrificial love.

The Power of Prayer

On my first night in prison, another inmate gave me a plastic rosary. I didn't know it then, but that rosary—and a renewed commitment to prayer—would become my greatest source of hope and strength during my incarceration.

I spent 807 days in prison, followed by thirty days in a community reentry house and four months on house arrest—a total of thirty-one months in custody with the Bureau of Prisons. Every day in custody, whether in prison, halfway house, or at home, I prayed the rosary—five decades, without fail. For those unfamiliar with it, the rosary is a form of ritual prayer structured around five sets of prayers: each set (or "decade") includes one Our Father, ten Hail Mary's, and one Glory Be. Each decade is accompanied by meditation on a "mystery" from Jesus' life, such as transforming water into wine at the wedding at Cana or his crucifixion. Rosary beads help keep track of the prayers as you meditate.

My parents prayed the rosary daily. Although I didn't appreciate their example at the time, imprisonment reawakened my own prayer life, which had been sporadic and inconsistent. Prison gave me time and motivation to explore both personal and communal prayer. The rosary provided structure, consistency, and focus. Although some find ritual prayer to be repetitive, it helped me to open my heart to God's presence and deepened my spiritual life.

Why did I start praying the rosary daily in prison? Simply because someone gave me one, and I kept going. Like Forrest Gump, who began running without knowing why, I started praying because I had lost everything—and prayer couldn't hurt. I continued because it gave meaning to my suffering.

At the San Diego Metropolitan Correctional Center, I prayed alone—except for a brief time when the MS-13 gang member, Miguel, joined me. When I was transferred to the Federal Transfer Center in Oklahoma City, I didn't have my beads, as they'd been packed with my personal belongings. But God gave me ten fingers, and that was enough. When I arrived at Florence Prison Camp in June 2013, I was reunited with my plastic rosary. My prayer life deepened. One day in the chapel, I came across a documentary about the life of St. Maximilian Kolbe. The film highlighted not just his martyrdom, but his devotion to Mary and the rosary. It inspired me to remain faithful to daily prayer and meditation on the mysteries of Christ.

I settled into a routine. I worked thirty-five hours a week at the prison motor pool as a dispatcher—a good job by camp standards—and spent the rest of my time reading, exercising, and praying. In the warmer months, I walked the track after dinner, saying the rosary as I moved silently through the Colorado twilight.

One evening, another inmate, Danny, approached and said he had noticed me walking each night with the rosary in hand. I told him it was part of my daily routine. He asked to join me. From then on, we walked the track together, praying the rosary most evenings throughout the summer of 2013.

Danny had once been CEO of a medical practice. He was serving a six-year sentence and was estranged from his family. Like me, he found healing in prayer. He was also a former enlisted Marine, and we bonded over our shared military experience. Initially, I thought I would be more focused if I prayed alone. I was wrong. While I valued solitary prayer, community prayer brought a new kind of spiritual depth. Danny and I became the founding members of what would grow into the Florence Camp rosary group. I don't know exactly how or why it grew so quickly, but it did. By the time I left the camp in May 2015, our group of fifteen to twenty men met in the chapel each evening.

The rosary group became my core community. Tony, a former police officer, joined later that summer. Then Ben, a former gang member and drug dealer, became a regular. We were an unlikely group—a retired Marine officer, a former CEO, a police commander, and a drug dealer—praying together every night. We held each other accountable not just in prayer, but in how we treated others.

Life in the prison camp followed a rhythm. My weekday began with breakfast, followed by seven hours of work. Each day the Bureau of Prisons conducts two "standing counts," one at 4 p.m. and another at 9 p.m. when all inmates must stand by their bunks while staff ensure everyone is accounted for. After the 4 p.m. count, I usually exercised outdoors, weather permitting. In the winter, we moved indoors. Every evening, after dinner, we gathered to pray. We always began with the rosary but our meetings often evolved into spirited conversations and mutual support. The prayer group became a sanctuary within the six-hundred-man camp.

Prison Politics

Life at the camp wasn't without violence or serious conflict. In prison culture, especially in higher-security institutions there's a term known as "prison politics." It refers to the self-segregation of inmates by race, a deeply ingrained system of unwritten rules. In California's state prisons, racial segregation was once formal policy. While the Federal Bureau of Prisons officially prohibits racial segregation, these "politics" still exist, even at minimum-security camps like Florence.

I encountered prison politics immediately, first at the Metropolitan Correctional Center in San Diego, then again upon arriving at Florence. After my first haircut—given by a Black inmate—another white inmate pulled me aside and told me I should get haircuts only from someone of my own race. I was stunned. The idea that my associations should be dictated by race seemed absurd, but it was part of the reality I had to navigate.

During my first six months, I clashed with these unspoken codes more than once, and it probably earned me a reputation for not playing by the rules. Fortunately, through God's grace and perhaps some luck, I avoided serious conflict. I was known as a Christian and a twenty-year Marine Corps veteran. I also made sure to display my own physical strength—I spent every opportunity at the weight pile and could bench press 315 pounds. It was partly for show. I wanted others to see me as someone seeking peace, but also capable of violence if pushed. That tension between being prayerful and projecting strength and toughness defined my time in prison.

When I arrived, the camp was severely overcrowded. Designed for 365 men, it housed nearly six hundred. One-man cells were shared by two or even three inmates. Some men lived in converted TV rooms. In 2013, the era of "Club Fed" was over. The Bureau of Prisons hit its peak population of 219,000, and overcrowding led to minimum-security camps housing individuals who might have been better placed elsewhere. Even in a camp like Florence, prison politics were very real. In December 2013, the camp erupted in a race riot between Black inmates and Southern Mexicans, known as Sureños. The fighting broke out on the yard and in the buildings, men used "locks in a sock," a common homemade weapon. I watched as two of my coworkers at the motor pool disposed of their weapons just before the camp went into total lockdown.

The violence was brutal. Several inmates were seriously injured. During lockdown, we were confined to our cells, food was delivered by staff, and all movement ceased. There were no visits, no recreation, no religious services. It was a harsh, joyless existence.

Yet, even during lockdown, our rosary group found a way to pray. Though we couldn't gather in the chapel, we prayed in small groups within our housing units. During the long weeks of isolation those brief evening prayers were often our only source of comfort. In hindsight, that period was spiritually significant. We checked in on one another and speculated how long the lockdown would last. Sadly, Christmas visits were canceled. My parents, brother, and sister-in-law had already traveled to Colorado to visit me. The Grinch didn't steal Christmas that year. Violence did.

There was, however, a silver lining. More than fifty inmates were transferred out, some for their direct involvement in the riot, others due to suspected gang ties. Those of us focused on rehabilitation and returning home felt relieved. The daily tension had been unbearable, but the atmosphere improved once the troublemakers were gone. After several weeks, the lockdown ended, and life returned to its normal rhythm. Though I witnessed other violent incidents during the remaining eighteen months at Florence, none matched the scale of the 2013 riot.

Living a Spiritual Life

I often tell people that going to prison was a spiritual blessing. In the United States, many of us live hectic lives, filling each day with responsibilities, distractions, and endless tasks. In a culture that emphasizes emotional, intellectual, and physical well-being, spiritual health is often neglected. Before prison, I was no exception. Balancing work, family, and other obligations left little time for spiritual reflection. My spiritual life consisted of attending Sunday Mass and occasionally praying, but there was little intentional growth. My excuse, like many others, was simple: there wasn't enough time.

Spirituality, at its core, is a recognition that something greater than ourselves exists. Christian spirituality calls us into a right relationship with God, especially through his Son, Jesus Christ. Though I was raised Catholic, attended Catholic schools, and remained active in my faith into adulthood, I hadn't truly developed an intimate, honest relationship with God. I practiced the faith, ensured my children received the sacraments, and occasionally volunteered. But I wasn't actively seeking spiritual transformation.

Greed and pride were obstacles to my own growth. I had claimed to want a Christ-centered life, especially after meeting Colette, but had only a superficial understanding of that life. Church attendance, meal prayers, and charitable giving were good practices, but they didn't necessarily reflect deep spiritual commitment. Only when I was physically arrested and removed from the busyness of daily life did I begin to experience real spiritual awakening.

Incarceration strips away everything: freedom, identity, relationships. You become invisible to most of the world. But prison also grants something rare—time. Time to think deeply, pray intentionally, and reflect on how you got there. Many, including me, were tempted to minimize or deny wrongdoing. I could have argued that my role in the crime was minor or that the government's case was overstated. But ultimately, my actions harmed others—especially my employees and my family. I had to accept responsibility and begin the hard work of understanding why I made such poor decisions. That honest reckoning marked the beginning of my spiritual growth.

During my incarceration, I discovered the power of both personal and communal prayer. My daily rosary ritual provided consistency, but prayer with others brought depth. Our rosary group began with four men: me, Danny, Tony, and Ben. Though from very different backgrounds, we became a spiritual community.

The Florence Federal Correctional Complex includes four facilities across fifty acres. The camp, a minimum-security unit, allows more freedom than the other institutions on site. Still, access to religious services was limited. Catholic services were provided by the Diocese of Pueblo. A priest came once a month, on a Wednesday, to celebrate Mass; a deacon came another Wednesday each month to lead a Communion service.

Although we were grateful, we longed to receive the Eucharist on Sundays, the heart of Catholic worship. Catholics believe that the Eucharist is the "source and summit" of their faith—that Christ is truly present in the consecrated bread and wine. We couldn't receive the Eucharist every Sunday, but we nourished our faith through Scripture, prayer, and an act of spiritual Communion. So, every Sunday morning, unless I had visitors, I participated in a peer-led Catholic prayer service. I often led the English-speaking group. I didn't seek that role; it seemed to unfold naturally, and I believe it was God's grace that allowed me to serve in that way. These moments reminded us that the Church exists wherever believers gather in faith.

My friend Tony and I took turns leading the Sunday services. Each week, I read the Mass readings and gospel ahead of time, preparing to offer a short reflection. Though I was comfortable speaking in professional settings, preaching the Word of God was different. At first, I was intimidated. But with time, and by God's grace, I found the courage to reflect on Scripture and speak to the thirty to forty men who gathered each Sunday. I didn't know it then, but this experience was preparing me for a future ministry in the Church—one I would take on years after my release.

The saying "absence makes the heart grow fonder" perfectly describes my relationship with the Eucharist during incarceration. We were fortunate to receive it twice a month—when the priest or deacon visited. But sometimes lockdowns, scheduling issues, or other disruptions meant we went weeks without it. We were always at the mercy of the institution, and inmates' access to sacraments wasn't a high priority.

That longing, combined with the repetition of spiritual communion prayers, deepened my appreciation for the Eucharist. To this day, the experience of missing the Sacrament makes receiving it more powerful. That absence continues to nourish my faith and reminds me of the gift Jesus gives us every time we gather at the table of the Lord.

Suffering and Spiritual Growth

Jesus, as a condemned prisoner, was publicly humiliated, mocked by his enemies and mourned by his loved ones. Crucifixion was one of the most barbaric and painful methods of execution, perfected by the Romans as a brutal deterrent to crime and rebellion. Christians believe his death was necessary to establish a new covenant with God and offer salvation to humanity.

Although our suffering may not compare to Jesus' passion and death, it can still be spiritually transformative. My time in prison, my own modest "passion," gave me the opportunity to renew my faith, deepen my understanding, and find the courage to share it with others.

The saints who endured great suffering are powerful models of resilience and faith. St. Dismas and St. Maximilian Kolbe show how suffering can lead to holiness. Both were prisoners, both endured injustice, and both are now venerated for their courage and faith. They remind us that God doesn't desire our suffering, but when it comes, he can use it to draw us closer to him.

The Greek word *metanoia* signifies a transformative change of heart and mind. It implies more than just regret or a surface-level shift—it's a deep, interior conversion. In the first chapter of Mark's Gospel, Jesus begins his ministry with this call: "The time is fulfilled, and the kingdom of God has come near; repent, and believe in the good news" (1:15). Catholics understand *metanoia* as a conversion that unites heart and mind in a new relationship with God. It's a transformation that turns us into true disciples of Jesus Christ.

The literal distance between the brain and the heart is about eighteen inches, but the spiritual gap between what we know and what we truly feel can be vast. When that distance is bridged—through grace—we experience *metanoia*, becoming new creations in Christ.

Often, suffering brings us to that point of conversion. Scripture is filled with stories of transformation born of hardship. The prophet Jonah fled from God's call and was swallowed by a great fish. In the depths—literally in the "belly of the beast"—he repented, changed, and resumed his mission. Prison is often referred to the same way—as the "belly of the beast." For me, prison became the place where I left behind self-centeredness and embraced a heart-centered spiritual life. I've since met many others who, in the solitude of a cell, experienced a similar rebirth—emotionally, spiritually, and morally.

My cellmate Tom was a fallen-away Catholic but remained devout in his Christian faith. He invited me to attend a weekly Protestant Bible study led by Fred and Wendy, a married couple who traveled from Colorado Springs to Florence every Thursday evening. Their presence was a gift—two people giving their time to help us grow spiritually. I initially joined out of respect for Tom, but soon became a regular participant. As the only Catholic in the group, I embodied the cliché that Catholics don't study the Bible. But the experience revealed how much Catholics and Protestants have in common. We studied Scripture together, and I began reading the Bible regularly—along with spiritual books that helped me better understand my faith. The Bible study group became another important part of my journey in prison.

I believe that without prison, my spiritual growth, then and now, would not have happened. As a father of four adult children, I don't want them to suffer. But I know they will face hardship, and I hope those challenges help them grow emotionally, intellectually, and spiritually. I imagine that God wants the same for each of us—though in a much deeper, eternal way. None of us can stay on the mountaintop forever. Life brings us into valleys—moments of difficulty, loss, and doubt. But in those valleys, we often find the richest lessons. Metanoia isn't just born of suffering. It requires our cooperation, our willingness to believe that a new way of being is possible. For those open to grace, prison can become a place of profound conversion.

These first two chapters have explored God's love for all people, including those society may consider undeserving. My reflections are more phenomenological than autobiographical. I offer them not simply as my story, but as a witness to a deeper truth. In the next chapter, we'll examine God's justice and how it compares to the American criminal justice system, particularly the development of the prison-industrial complex. That chapter will take a critical look at corrections in the United States and explore how the system often fails to reflect the values Christians and citizens claim to hold.

Chapter 3

Justice and Mercy

Justice as a Virtue

Catholicism recognizes four cardinal virtues that guide us toward holiness: prudence, justice, courage, and temperance. All other virtues stem from these four, which provide moral and ethical standards for living rightly. These cardinal virtues are derived from both Scripture and Greek philosophy, notably from Plato and Aristotle. This chapter will examine the virtue of justice as it relates to crime and punishment and explore how all are called to ensure justice for every member of society.

In both the Old and New Testaments, justice is often synonymous with righteousness. In the Book of Wisdom, the cardinal virtues are named as essential for a rightly ordered moral life: "And if anyone loves righteousness, her labors are virtues; for she teaches self-control and prudence, justice and courage; nothing in life is more profitable for mortals than these" (Ws 8:7). Virtues serve as guideposts for the People of God as well as for all members of civil society. It is common to distinguish between Old Testament justice, which is said to be harsher and more unforgiving, than New Testament justice. This may appear to be so under a literal interpretation of scripture, but as a Catholic I seek to understand the Bible in context, considering both its literary form and its message.

Old Testament justice is often associated with the phrase "an eye for an eye" from the Book of Exodus. This principle, known as *lex talionis*, was an ancient Near Eastern legal standard of proportionality. Catholics do not interpret "eye for an eye" literally. Rather, lex talionis emphasized restraint and proportionality, discouraging vengeance. Biblical justice sought to restore balance by making amends—restitution—and, more importantly, by repairing relationships.

Howard Zehr, in his foundational restorative justice book *Changing Lenses*, discusses the Jewish concept of *Shalom* as a way of living. While commonly translated as "peace," Shalom carries a much deeper meaning. Central to the Torah, it represents a way of living together in harmony. When that harmony is broken, justice restores order and makes things right again. This concept, not unique to the Jewish people, reflected the approach to peace and justice shared by many ancient cultures, including the Indigenous peoples of the Americas.

Jesus Provides Justice

As a Catholic I believe that God is love, and his perfect love is revealed through the Incarnation. Jesus' dwelling among us, fully human and fully divine, is the ultimate expression of that love. Through his life, Jesus modeled forgiveness, mercy, and justice. His teachings and miracles showed that true justice is perfected through mercy and forgiveness.

The Incarnation fulfilled salvation history. Jesus completed God's promise to the Israelites and to all humanity by offering salvation and eternal life. In the Old Testament, justice was often viewed as transactional and rigid, leaving little room for mercy. In contrast, Jesus embodied divine justice infused with mercy, love, and forgiveness. Yet, even those who claim to be God's people, still struggle to embrace this model, often reverting to the stricter justice of the Old Testament. The tension between Old and New Testament justice did not end with Jesus' coming; humanity, especially those in positions of power, still cling to retributive justice rather than the compassionate justice of Christ.

The Gospel of John recounts Jesus' encounter with a woman caught in adultery. According to the law, the community had the right to execute her by stoning. Jesus does not challenge the law or demand a lesser punishment. Instead, he offers a profound challenge: "Let anyone among you who is without sin be the first to throw a stone at her" (Jn 8:7). As Jesus writes in the dirt, perhaps listing the sins of her accusers, his words convict their hearts. One by one, they drop their stones and walk away. Left alone with the woman, Jesus does not condemn her but calls her to accountability: "Go your way, and from now on do not sin again."

This story reveals an often-overlooked dimension of divine justice. Human justice typically focuses on punishment—asking what happened, who is responsible, and what penalty is deserved. God's justice, however, seeks not to punish, but to make things right. Sometimes punishment, is necessary, but it often does not heal the harm caused by wrongdoing. True justice must restore relationships and promote healing for victims, offenders, and the broader community. Punishment has value only if it opens the path to reconciliation, mercy, and transformation. Jesus transcended the "eye for an eye" model that for centuries guided Jewish law. That model emphasized proportionality, but Jesus emphasizes restoration. His justice includes accountability but also offers mercy and the possibility of renewal within the community.

The parable of the Good Samaritan illustrates this perfectly. A man, beaten and robbed on the road to Jericho, is ignored by two passersby, including a priest. A Samaritan, to Jews an outsider, stops to help, tends the man's wounds, provides shelter, and promises to pay for his continued care. The Samaritan acts with mercy and compassion, embodying what it means to be a true neighbor. With this parable, Jesus teaches his followers to care for those who suffer harm and to seek healing and restoration for all involved, including those who cause harm. The Samaritan, though socially marginalized, becomes the model of Christlike justice—one rooted in mercy, compassion, and love.

We learn nothing more about the robbers in the story, but we can assume that Jesus would hold them accountable while also extending mercy and offering a path to forgiveness. God's love encompasses both the victim and the offender. Jesus' encounter with the adulterous woman and the parable of the Good Samaritan, provide the People of God with a model of justice that focuses on reconciliation, restoration, and healing. Our modern justice system shows how far the usual practices can stray from this divine model. Mercy and forgiveness are too often absent from the pursuit of justice.

Justice without Integrity

The U.S. criminal justice system can be divided broadly into three parts: law enforcement, prosecution and courts, and corrections. The first two chapters, presented my experiences with the corrections system. This section, will describe my experience with the prosecution and the courts.

The federal criminal justice system in the United States is often extremely punitive, allowing little room for leniency. When I learned in January 2011 that I was the target of a federal investigation, I initially cooperated with the U.S. Attorney's Office and the investigating agencies. I hired a criminal defense attorney from Los Angeles to represent me and another from San Diego to represent my business. I intended to cooperate fully and provide all the necessary information to mitigate my role in what the government described as a conspiracy.

I met with the assistant U.S. attorneys and several federal investigators during a "Queen for a Day" session, which allowed me to answer questions and share my side of the story. A "Queen for a Day," also known as a "Proffer" or "Proffer Letter," is a written agreement to conduct an informal interview between the federal prosecutors and a suspect or criminal defendant regarding information and evidence relevant to some criminal activity. The defendant's or suspect's goal in the proffer is to provide useful information to the prosecutor in order to garner leniency and cut a deal (usually a favorable sentence recommendation such as probation) with the federal government. The prosecutor's goal is to obtain useful information from the suspect that would support the investigation and assist in convicting other persons involved in the crime. It is important that the suspect be honest and truthful during the proffer interview. In exchange for cooperation and providing information, the prosecutor pledges not to use the proffer information against the suspect or defendant in later court proceedings.

My attorney believed the meeting went well; the prosecutors even remarked that they believed I had been truthful. At that time, I still did not think I had broken the law. I viewed my involvement as minimal and thought the government would see that I had no criminal intent. I believed I had been exploited by corrupt contracting officers and government employees who used my business and others for personal gain. In hindsight, I failed to recognize how my own greed and arrogance contributed to poor decisions that enabled others—and myself—to profit from a criminal scheme.

What exactly was my involvement in the criminal conspiracy? My company, a small industrial tool and supply firm in San Diego County, sold industrial products to local manufacturers and the Department of Defense. After the 2008 recession, local manufacturing declined, but defense spending rose due to the Global War on Terrorism. By 2009–2010, about 75 percent of our business came from our primary customer, the Department of Defense.

We held several contracts with the Department of the Navy to supply tools and equipment to the aircraft repair facility at Naval Air Station North Island. These contracts were inherited from the previous owners, one of whom continued managing them after I purchased the business. One of these—what I call the "bad contract"—covered aircraft consumable parts, items used up during maintenance and typically not tracked. Unbeknownst to me, the contract was written with the intention to allow government officials to add items beyond the agreed-upon schedule—everything from general tools to "quality of life" items for workers.

About a year into ownership of our company, I realized the extent of the off-contract purchases. My legal exposure at that point was minor, but I allowed the practice within my company to continue. Greed, arrogance, and naïveté led me to believe that breaking the law was justified under the banner of "the customer is always right." I did not recognize that multiple schemes between government contracting officials and local defense companies were operating at the same time.

My father's saying, "You can't do the right thing by doing the wrong thing" proved true here. I justified these actions as good customer service, fulfilling urgent needs without bureaucratic delays. In reality, however, the lack of oversight denied other companies' fair competition. It was wrong—and illegal. Admitting and fully understanding my culpability took years, even after my release from prison. Accepting responsibility was the first step toward healing and reintegration. That lesson came at a great personal cost to me and my family but also brought a renewed sense of moral clarity. I have vowed never again to sacrifice my principles for money or anyone else.

I had no excuses for my actions or my ignorance of government contracting law. As president, I was responsible for everything my company did. Yet the government's conduct in investigating and prosecuting my case was also deeply flawed. Prosecutors portrayed the case as small contractors defrauding the government out of millions, when in truth, government employees had orchestrated multiple schemes for personal enrichment. The evidence supported this, but the U.S. Attorney's Office ignored it, showing a lack of integrity in not presenting the case honestly. I broke the law, and so did others, but the narrative the government told was false.

In the federal criminal justice system, 97 percent of cases end in plea bargains, and of the 3 percent that go to trial, about two-thirds result in convictions. In total, roughly 99 percent of federal defendants are found guilty, either through plea or trial. Against overwhelming government resources, most defendants cannot afford a proper defense. About 95 percent of cases, both state and federal, end this way, making jury trials exceedingly rare.

For more than a year I cooperated with investigators, meeting with prosecutors to explain my role. Thirteen people were eventually charged, including government employees and owners of four local businesses. Eleven pled guilty. Two of us—I and one other—did not. You might ask why. Even when admitting I had broken the law, I remained in denial about my intent. I convinced myself that I was not truly guilty. It was faulty reasoning, especially in light of the government's determination to hold me accountable.

A plea bargain, a negotiated agreement between the government and a defendant to admit guilt in exchange for reduced charges, fines, or prison time, benefits both sides by saving time and money. Over a year after I learned I was under investigation—I received a plea offer. In January 2011 federal agents had already raided my home and business, seizing my assets and accounts. In spring 2012, prosecutors offered a plea to two charges: conspiracy to commit wire fraud and tax fraud. My attorney said the likely sentence would be eighteen to thirty months in prison plus restitution for government losses.

I understood the conspiracy charge. It broadly applied to my company's actions. Although I maintained that I lacked intent to defraud the government, I knew laws had been broken. I could not, however, accept the tax fraud charge. I had always followed my tax advisor's guidance and avoided questionable deductions. My attorney explained that the IRS Criminal Investigative Division (IRS CID) wanted credit for a conviction, even if the charge was unrelated to the facts. This information soured my relationship with the government and my attorney, and I became less cooperative.

When my attorney asked the U.S. Attorney's Office to remove the tax charge, they agreed but replaced it with a money laundering charge, again to satisfy IRS CID agency's desire to receive credit for a conviction. At that point, I realized the government was more interested in closing the case than pursuing justice. They wanted me to lie under oath to fit their narrative. I refused. My moral clarity was finally returning—too late to undo past mistakes, but just in time to guide my next steps.

The plea-bargaining system, in my experience, is coercive. Defendants are pressured to accept false or exaggerated charges to expedite cases. They must swear under oath that their plea is truthful. I could not do that.

There was no evidence that I had committed tax fraud or money laundering. Even my attorney admitted as much, though he seemed resigned to the process. So, I stopped cooperating, fired my attorney, and knowing the risk prepared to face trial.

At certain times in a person's life their soul is truly challenged. My moment came when I stopped cooperating with the government and decided to proceed to a trial. I could have continued to cooperate, swear under oath to whatever charges the government asked me to plead, and in return receive a lenient sentence. I knew that if I was found guilty, not cooperating meant up to twenty years in prison. But I also knew that if I did capitulate and agree I would become a different man; I chose to reclaim the moral compass that guided me for most of my adult life. I committed to doing what I believed was the right course of action, understanding the consequences could be more severe. I could not explain to my children that in order to reduce a prison sentence I cooperated with the system, by accepting a plea bargain not based on the truth. In other words, I would have to tell my kids that I lied to get a better deal. This just was not me.

Out of pragmatic realism, my wife urged me to accept the plea in hopes of leniency. She and I both knew that refusing a plea could increase my potential sentence from a few years to as many as twenty. Still, I could not lie for a lighter punishment. I could not face my children knowing I had done so. Once I explained my reasoning, Colette's understanding and support changed everything. She became my strongest supporter. Her courage and steadfastness kept our family together through the years that followed.

A New Lawyer and an Indictment

One of my former Marine Corps commanding officers recommended a highly respected criminal defense attorney in Orange County, California. My former boss and I drove about ninety miles north to meet Kevin Barry McDermott, a criminal trial lawyer and former Marine Corps attorney. When I hired my first lawyer, I didn't realize the significant difference between a trial attorney and other types of lawyers. Kevin's reputation was exceptional. He had tried more than two hundred cases. Before agreeing to represent me, he wanted to meet my wife. About a week later, after Colette and I spoke with him, Kevin agreed to take my case.

For the first time in nearly eighteen months, we felt a measure of hope. Kevin, known as "The War Lawyer," was relentless. The nickname, which suited him well, mirrored how I began to see my own situation. With limited resources, one skilled attorney, and the support of my family, I was going to war with the U.S. government. Bullets weren't flying, but the consequences were still life-altering.

In August 2012, my indictment was unsealed, and I appeared before a federal magistrate. Kevin and I learned that I faced a seven-count indictment, including conspiracy to commit wire fraud, bribery, and money laundering, along with individual bribery charges. Interestingly, the government dropped the tax fraud charge. Kevin explained they had no evidence to support it. By being formally indicted we gained an advantage, access to discovery, the body of evidence the prosecution planned to use at trial. Until that point, I had little idea how the government could prove me criminally liable.

With Kevin's help, we came to understand clearly the case against me. My trial, alongside one co-defendant, the owner of another local tool and supply company, was set to begin in roughly six months. Our judge, the Honorable Larry Burns, was reputed to be fair but firm. Generally, court proceedings move slowly, but Judge Burns was known as a "docket rocket" who wanted to resolve cases quickly and efficiently. I was relieved that my case would proceed sooner rather than later; I wanted to face the uncertainty head-on and begin rebuilding my life.

Kevin warned me that a jury trial would be the most difficult challenge of my life. As a fellow Marine who had represented many veterans, he told me that not even combat could prepare me for the emotional strain of standing trial and facing a potential loss of liberty. He was right.

In the fall of 2012, while preparing for trial, I was taking three courses in a doctoral program at the University of San Diego. In addition to that pressure, I was now spending twenty to thirty hours a week reviewing over nine thousand pages of discovery. Most of the evidence pertained not to me or my company but to other co-defendants. The most serious allegations against me were specific bribery charges carrying up to fifteen years in prison each. Interestingly, both my co-defendant and I faced the same number of charges—seven. That seems to be the federal prosecutors' template.

At first, I believed my legal exposure was limited only to allowing my company to fulfill off-contract requests. But as I reviewed the evidence, I began to see the full extent of the corruption in which my company was enmeshed. One company had bought a $43,000 BMW for a government official. As a Christmas gift another had given a $20,000 cash bribe. The crushing emotional weight of these details made me physically ill. As a retired Marine Corps officer, I valued integrity above all else, yet I was now fighting charges that placed me among the corrupt.

A Dark Moment

In October 2012, I attended the hearing at which seven co-defendants who had already pled guilty appeared before Judge Burns for sentencing. One of them was my employee who managed our government sales and contracts. By accepting plea bargains, all these defendants were expected to cooperate with the government against me and the one remaining co-defendant.

During the lengthy session, each defendant addressed the court, accepted responsibility, and spoke before sentencing. The prosecution presented an overview of the case, still portraying the conspiracy as one driven not by the corrupt government employees who were the architects and primary beneficiaries of the scheme, but by greedy defense contractors. This misrepresentation was significant because it led the judge to decide their sentences largely based upon the prosecution's narrative.

Judge Burns sentenced the defendants to various prison terms, ranging from thirty weekends in custody to forty-one months in prison. Given what I had learned after reviewing the discovery, I thought these sentences actually were lenient. The harshest sentence, forty-one months, went to a government employee who had engaged in kickback schemes worth more than $500,000 over fifteen years. His attorney noted that he had recently been baptized as a Christian before sentencing, which personally irked me, knowing this particular government employee was the architect for the entire scheme and had bilked the government out of hundreds of thousands of dollars for his personal benefit.

True to his reputation, Judge Burns immediately remanded most of the defendants into custody after sentencing. Watching that moment had a profound effect. I realized that within months, if I were found guilty at trial, I could be in their place.

I left the courtroom angry, ashamed, anxious, and afraid. I don't even remember driving home. The mix of emotions triggered a full-blown panic attack, and I ended up in Coronado at the Sharp Hospital emergency room. While the medical staff checked my vitals, I muttered something about jumping off the Coronado Bay Bridge. I left the hospital against medical advice. My departure and my comment prompted an immediate response.

When I arrived home, several police cars were waiting, along with my deeply worried parents and wife. I was taken into custody under what's known as a 5150, which authorizes law enforcement to place someone experiencing a mental health crisis into involuntary psychiatric care for up to seventy-two hours. I was admitted to the Naval Hospital in San Diego for evaluation.

During the previous twenty-one months of legal turmoil, I thought I had already reached my lowest point, but this was my personal "Death Valley." I was supposed to be attending classes and preparing for trial, yet I found myself under suicide watch. Ironically, I felt more shame about my breakdown than about being indicted or later incarcerated. In our society, the stigma surrounding mental illness remains powerful, but it's important to acknowledge the human emotional and psychological toll of the criminal justice process.

I spent three days in the hospital. The doctors determined I was emotionally fragile, but not suicidal. My family and friends were deeply concerned, but I was more focused on keeping others from finding out about my hospitalization. In hindsight, this experience marked a turning point. It deepened my compassion and understanding for those suffering from trauma, shame, and despair. One of my closest friends from the Marine Corps, after returning from combat, had taken his own life. He had seemed unshakable—strong, confident, larger than life—but he was silently struggling. He needed help and didn't know how to ask. I now understand that pain more clearly. My own breakdown, though brief, became a blessing in disguise. It reminded me of the importance of vulnerability, faith, and the grace of having people who love and support you when you need it most.

Punishment Is the Focus in the System

The American criminal justice system operates primarily on the principle of retributive justice, which focuses on repayment for wrongdoing, most often through incarceration. Few Americans fully grasp the extent of this punitive system. The facts speak for themselves: at any given time the United States imprisons more than two million people, the highest incarceration rate in the world—about six hundred per one hundred thousand residents. With less than 5 percent of the world's population, the U.S. holds roughly 22 percent of its prisoners.

This system rarely reflects the universal virtues of love, forgiveness, and mercy. In many ways, our time is not unlike the era when Jesus lived under the authority of the Roman Empire. Like Rome, our modern state wields immense power over individuals—especially in matters of justice. We often take pride in being "a nation of laws," and rightly so. Yet as Christians, we must remember that God calls us not only to uphold the law but also to live out compassion, love, and mercy in our institutions and communities.

We are commanded to build a society that mirrors the justice of Christ—one that integrates mercy into its structures and values. Punishment, though often necessary, should never be the ultimate goal of justice. Its true purpose is to acknowledge harm, deter wrongdoing, and create opportunities for repentance, healing, and reintegration.

God's mercy is infinitely greater than his punishment. Divine justice always prioritizes forgiveness and renewal, even when accountability is required. In the next chapter, I will share an alternative approach to justice—one that reflects God's mercy more closely—and describe a personal experience in which I received unexpected compassion from one of the least likely sources.

Chapter 4

Restorative Justice is Jesus' Justice

A Punitive System of Justice

The U.S. legal system is rooted in English Common Law, which relies on past court rulings, or precedents. This adversarial system of justice offers several advantages. Chief among them is the guarantee of due process, which requires the government to act according to established laws and legal principles. The Fourteenth Amendment's due process clause protects citizens from losing their liberty without a fair hearing.

Ideally, our legal system safeguards individuals from being deprived of freedom without their day in court. Yet, in practice, the adversarial system often prioritizes winning cases over the shared duty of both defense and prosecution to seek justice. What was designed to ensure fairness has, in many ways, become a contest between victory and defeat. Although the U.S. justice system is often hailed as one of the most sophisticated in the world, the reality is more nuanced: it produces the highest incarceration rate globally and is also the most expensive. Most of those accused never go to trial because they lack the resources to mount a strong defense. Instead, plea bargains, often unjust or coerced, become the default resolution.

Why is the U.S. criminal justice system so punitive? The country's exceptionally high incarceration rate suggests that in America punishment, rather than rehabilitation, defines justice. From the end of the Civil War until the late 1960s, incarceration rates remained steady, about two hundred inmates per one hundred thousand people. For much of that period, correctional goals emphasized rehabilitation and restoring individuals as productive citizens. But beginning in the 1960s, a shift in public sentiment and legislation paved the way for mass incarceration.

Crime rates that began rising in the 1960s continued climbing until the early 1990s. In the early 1970's, sociologist Robert Martinson published a massive study that concluded that rehabilitation programs for inmates produced few positive results. His findings popularized the "nothing works" doctrine, leading policymakers to abandon rehabilitation as a primary goal. Public fear of rising crime, coupled with the growing problem of illicit drug use—especially among youth—fueled support for harsher penalties.

The "War on Drugs," launched in the 1970s under President Nixon, intensified during the 1980s with the Reagan Administration as the crack cocaine epidemic ravaged U.S. cities. These laws resulted in the incarceration rate doubling between 1970 and 1990. Ironically, when crime rates began to decline, Congress passed the 1994 Clinton Crime Bill, the largest crime legislation in U.S. history. Backed by bipartisan support, it allocated nearly ten billion dollars to hire one hundred thousand police officers and build new prisons. The political lesson was clear: being "tough on crime" wins votes.

Crime, more than most policy issues, provokes strong emotions and moral reactions. One of government's core responsibilities is to protect its citizens from internal and external threats. When crime rates rise—or are perceived to rise—public demand for immediate action often triggers a "moral panic," prompting reactive laws that do little to address root causes. Moral panics regarding crime have led to bad policy by lawmakers.

The media amplifies this cycle by sensationalizing violent or noteworthy crimes. Even when statistics show overall declines, a single high-profile case can dominate headlines and pressure lawmakers to "do something." The 1994 Crime Bill exemplified this dynamic: passed amid falling crime rates, within a decade it nonetheless doubled the incarceration rate. By the early 2000s, more than 750 Americans per one hundred thousand were imprisoned, and another five million were under supervision through probation or parole. Today, over eighty million Americans have a criminal record, with nineteen million bearing felony convictions.

Recent reforms have sought to correct these excesses, some with bipartisan support. Yet spikes in crime during and after the COVID-19 pandemic rekindled public fear, reigniting calls for harsher penalties. U.S. criminal justice policy seems to swing perpetually between leniency and severity. Our punitive system of justice comes about when lawmakers yield to constituents' demands for tough approaches to crime and punishment. Politically, being punitive remains the safer stance—even though data consistently show that restorative and rehabilitative approaches yield better results.

The U.S. system's roots in English law make comparisons with the United Kingdom illuminating. Despite their shared heritage, the U.K.'s incarceration rate is about 75 percent lower. Canada and most European nations imprison even fewer people—roughly 85 percent less than the U.S.—and focus on rehabilitation and reintegration. Their recidivism rates are also far lower. Norway, for instance, reincarcerates only 20 percent of released prisoners within two years, compared to 50 percent in the U.S. Norwegian prisons prioritize accountability and reintegration from the outset.

Over the past five decades, the U.S. justice system has grown increasingly punitive, while comparable Western nations have emphasized restoration—for victims, offenders, and communities alike. In Europe, incarceration holds offenders accountable for harm, but it marks the beginning, not the end, of the restorative process. Countries like Canada, Norway, and others achieve longer-lasting public safety, lower recidivism, and more cost-effective justice. By contrast, America's punitive model is not only more expensive but also less effective at reducing crime or promoting healing.

Trial Preparation

I spent the final months of 2012 preparing for my trial. In December I completed the fall semester of my graduate studies and notified the university that for the spring semester I would take a leave of absence. I hoped to return as a full-time student that summer. Nearly two years had passed since federal agents executed a search warrant, seized company funds, and informed me that I was the target of an investigation.

For the first eighteen months after receiving the target letter, only a few close family members and friends knew about my legal troubles. After my indictment, my wife and I began informing our wider circle that I would stand trial in 2013. Our four children did not learn of my situation until the indictment in August 2012. Sitting them down to explain was one of the most difficult conversations of my life. I told them what had happened, took responsibility, and reassured them that, whatever the outcome, we would face it together as a family. We did our best to provide them and the rest of our family with hope.

I barely remember Christmas of 2012. My attention was entirely consumed by trial preparation for the following February. During this uncertain period, Colette and my parents, who lived with us at the time, were incredibly supportive. My attorney, Kevin, provided much-needed confidence and optimism. At his direction, I wrote a trial brief summarizing my entire case from my perspective, which was submitted to both the judge and the prosecution. Writing it proved cathartic—it forced me to confront my own culpability and to identify inaccuracies in the government's narrative.

A few weeks before trial, the government made a final plea offer, a standard tactic, since prosecutors typically avoid trials if they can. They claimed to have a "smoking gun": a video showing me giving a government employee a watch, which they argued was proof of bribery. Ironically, the reality was the opposite. One of my employees had received the watch from a contracting officer who said it was surplus property. Government employees were apparently gifting each other such items, though I was unaware of it.

When I learned about the gift, I told my employee he could not keep it and that it had to be returned. I personally returned the watch, unaware that I was being recorded. The government had been surveilling corrupt contracting officers for months, and I was caught on video not violating proper procedure but following it. At the time, contractors could give government employees gifts valued at up to forty dollars, enough to cover a business lunch. The watch, worth about $250, far exceeded that limit. Despite my explanation, the government dismissed my account, and I rejected their plea offer. At that point, neither side was willing to listen.

Before any trial, both sides typically file pretrial motions. Kevin and I appeared before Judge Burns several times for these hearings. At one point, Kevin deliberately stood between the judge and me to block my facial expressions. He later told me I looked defiant—an "F-you face," as he put it—which would not help my case. Both he and Colette urged me to appear calmer and more approachable during trial. Although I didn't wear glasses at the time, Colette bought me a pair to soften my appearance. It amused me at first, but I came to understand that a jury trial is partly theater: the facts matter but so does how the defendant is perceived. The glasses worked.

The Trial Begins

My trial took place in the downtown San Diego federal courthouse, on the fourteenth floor. Kevin, stayed at the Navy Lodge on North Island in Coronado—an affordable and modest choice that reflected his professionalism and care. On the first day, my father and I picked him up, crossed the Coronado Bay Bridge, and drove to the courthouse. Dressed in a blue sport coat, tie, slacks, and my new glasses, I felt the weight of uncertainty pressing on me throughout that surreal morning.

The trial began with *voir dire* also known as jury selection, in which potential jurors are examined by the judge, prosecution, and defense. Forty citizens were called. Each side could question them and make peremptory challenges—dismissals without cause, except for race or gender. The prosecution had six such challenges; the defense had ten.

Kevin brought in Aaron Meyer, a young criminal defense attorney and former Marine, to assist during voir dire. Aaron had recently left the Marine Corps and under Kevin's mentorship was beginning private practice. Having two former Marines on my team inspired confidence; they shared a sense of discipline, loyalty, and integrity that resonated deeply with me. Aaron's insight proved invaluable, and both he and Kevin remain close friends to this day.

By the end of the first day, twelve jurors and two alternates were seated. Although the Constitution guarantees a "jury of one's peers," few, if any, of the jurors had experience with government contracting, small business ownership, or procurement rules—the very heart of my case. This lack of technical understanding could have worked for or against me, depending on how the evidence was presented. Until I was able to review thousands of pages of discovery or evidence, I myself did not fully understand the sophistication of the criminal conspiracy and the mechanisms that government employees used to defraud the government. The jury would not be afforded the same opportunity to digest all the evidence and understand the mechanisms that allowed the government employees to defraud the government.

Including jury selection, the trial lasted six days. Judge Burns was known for running a tight courtroom. One co-defendant was tried alongside me, and Kevin considered filing a motion to separate our cases. But because Judge Burns was unlikely to approve it, our strategy instead was to let the prosecution focus on my co-defendant, whose evidence was far more damaging. The plan worked: roughly 70 percent of the prosecution's time centered on her.

Once the jury was sworn in, both sides delivered opening statements. The prosecution always goes first, followed by the defense. Two assistant U.S. attorneys presented the government's case; both were relatively inexperienced with jury trials, since most federal cases are settled via plea deals rather than jury trials. In contrast, Kevin had tried over two hundred jury cases, and my co-defendant's attorney was also highly skilled. The difference in courtroom experience was striking.

The prosecution's main witnesses were co-defendants in the conspiracy, many already sentenced and incarcerated. They had agreed to cooperate in exchange for possible sentence reductions under Rule 35 of the Federal Rules of Criminal Procedure, which allows judges to lower sentences for "substantial assistance." This incentive gave them every reason to testify in ways favorable to the government. On the stand, two witnesses who had previously told the FBI they didn't know me suddenly claimed otherwise. Kevin's cross-examination dismantled their credibility.

While the prosecutors lacked trial experience, they had the full resources of the U.S. Department of Justice behind them. Jurors, being human, often assume that if the government brings charges, the defendant must be guilty. The defense must therefore remind them of the most fundamental principle of our system: the presumption of innocence.

Each witness the government called reinforced the prosecution's narrative of conspiracy and bribery. Kevin, however, masterfully cross-examined each one, exposing inconsistencies and highlighting testimony that supported my innocence. The ringleader of the corruption scheme, a government employee, even admitted under cross-examination that I had never offered bribes or been involved in any of his wrongdoing. The government didn't even question the employee who had received the returned watch that was supposedly their "smoking gun"—likely fearing the truth would contradict their narrative. Things were looking good for Team Ehnow.

The prosecution's star witness against me, my former employee and business partner, had been sentenced to eighteen months in prison and was incarcerated at the time of the trial. On direct examination, his statements about my involvement were vague and speculative—he repeatedly said, "I suspect he knew." Those words, full of uncertainty, left plenty of room for reasonable doubt. I felt optimistic that the jury too, would believe that there was reasonable doubt regarding my own guilt. Hearing him testify against me was painful; I had once trusted him deeply, both professionally and personally. After the prosecution rested, the defense had options. We could rest our case entirely and argue that the government hadn't met its burden of proof, or we could make a motion for acquittal under Rule 29. Kevin and my co-defendant's attorney did make a motion for acquittal under Rule 29, but Judge Burns denied the motion, so we moved to our next plan. We would present our own defense, including seven character witnesses, and I would take the stand.

Taking the Stand and Jury Deliberations

Kevin and I debated whether I should testify. The prosecution's case against me was weak, and Kevin's cross-examinations had gone extremely well. Most of the prosecution's case was focused on my co-defendant, and as Kevin predicted, it made me appear as a peripheral player in the scheme. The few audio recordings that the government played for the jury suggested that I had some exposure to the conspiracy, but I believed they did not indicate any criminal intent or significant involvement in it. Going into the defense presentation our case was pretty solid. Still, I wanted to speak directly to the jury. I needed them to hear my story in my own words.

The risk of testifying, of course, is the prosecution's opportunity for cross-examination. Kevin questioned me for more than an hour, allowing me to clarify facts and show that I had no criminal intent. Then the prosecution cross-examined me for a couple of hours. I answered confidently and truthfully, maintaining composure even under pressure. I believe my testimony helped my case; it allowed the jury to see me not as a caricature of guilt, but as a human being.

After I testified, Kevin called seven-character witnesses—each chosen strategically to reflect different aspects of my life: a company employee, two former commanding officers, a Catholic deacon, and lifelong friends.

Their testimony emphasized my integrity, faith, and service to others. Kevin's defense presentation was outstanding, and at the time I thought it was going to exonerate me completely.

During closing arguments, the defense goes first. The prosecution closed by stating that it "did not matter whether Mr. Ehnow knew he was breaking the law, only that he broke it." That statement, I thought, effectively conceded the issue of criminal intent. As before, their focus was mostly on my co-defendant. When the arguments ended, Judge Burns instructed the jury and sent them to deliberate. Deliberations stretched over a weekend. That Friday evening, my family, friends, and I gathered with Kevin at a nearby bar, cautiously optimistic and in a somewhat celebratory mood. Everyone believed there was a strong chance of acquittal. For the first time in two years, I allowed myself a glimpse of hope.

On Monday, March 4, 2013 we returned to court. The jury asked to review audio recordings between my former employee and business partner and me, conversations about a pending invoice between my company and the government. They wanted to hear the entire exchange, which made me somewhat worried. Any time the jury asks to review evidence it is not good news for the defense. Those recordings stemmed from wiretaps authorized during the government's 2009–2010 investigation. Though I was never the subject of a wiretap, one of my employees was. Under Title III of the Omnibus Crime Control and Safe Streets Act of 1968, wiretaps require a judge's approval and are supposed to be used only when "all other investigative means have been exhausted." In practice, more than 90 percent of requests are approved. My company had detailed records of all transactions, so investigators could have easily obtained the same information through an audit—no wiretap necessary. But no one seemed to care about that.

Title III wiretaps, originally used for organized crime, in the 1980's and 1990's were greatly expanded to include all types of white-collar and other crimes. Unfortunately, judges often "rubber stamp" approval of wiretaps. In my case, my company kept detailed records and receipts of all transactions with the government, and all contracts are subject to an annual audit. At any time, the government agencies could have requested all information and receipts for all contracts or conducted an audit, but they never did. The government investigating agencies never took the time to request an audit or obtain information about our business through ordinary means. The quick approval of wiretaps without exhausting other venues to obtain information was problematic, and it remains so as an investigative tool by the government.

The recording in question involved a $65,000 invoice for a HAAS CNC machine and aircraft equipment racks—legitimate items delivered under contract. The government later claimed this was outside the contract's scope, though contracting officials themselves had added the relevant line item. On the tape, I told my employee I didn't care how he listed the items as long as the invoice was paid. We had already spent $50,000 on equipment. The government, misunderstanding the context, portrayed this as furthering the conspiracy. Without the context, the audio sounded incriminating against me. Unfortunately, the jury agreed.

That afternoon, the jury reached its verdict. My co-defendant was found guilty on six of seven counts. I was found guilty on two: conspiracy to commit wire fraud and one count of bribery. I handed my watch and wallet to Kevin as U.S. Marshals led me away. I was now an inmate.

Awaiting Sentencing

I spent my first night in custody in a private detention facility in downtown San Diego run by the GEO Group. This private prison houses federal detainees, including undocumented immigrants. During my medical intake, I informed the nurse practitioner that I had a blood disease requiring daily medications, including the chemotherapy drug Gleevec. The medical staff told me they could not provide those medications. The GEO facility simply didn't know how to handle my medical condition. Early the next morning, I was transported to Alvarado Medical Center and for the next forty-eight hours I was handcuffed to a hospital bed. While I was hospitalized, a correctional officer remained in my room around the clock. During my stay, my roommate—another inmate—died of natural causes. Under the guard's watchful eye the staff placed his body in a bag and wheeled him away. I spent the rest of my time there alone, with only the officer for company. He wasn't much of a conversationalist.

Meanwhile, Colette was enduring her own nightmare. As both a physician and my wife, her greatest concern was getting my medication to me. Neither she nor Kevin could determine where I had been taken. Desperate, she walked to both the Metropolitan Correctional Center and the GEO prison, only to be turned away at each. No one would confirm my location or provide information about my condition. That night, Colette wept in frustration and fear, unsure whether I was safe or receiving the care I needed. Even now, my heart sinks when I recall her anguish during those two days of uncertainty.

Eventually, the hospital determined my medications, and I was transferred to the MCC to await sentencing. Federal rules require a minimum of twelve weeks between a guilty verdict and sentencing. True to his reputation for timeliness, Judge Burns scheduled my hearing for May 20, 2013, exactly twelve weeks after my conviction. Kevin immediately began gathering letters of support from family, friends, colleagues, and others. He compiled more than sixty-five letters to submit to the court, but Judge Burns requested that only ten be submitted to him. Though I was grieving the loss of my freedom, reading the letters—especially one from my eldest son, Brendan—deeply moved me. His plea for leniency so he could continue spending time with his father was almost too painful to bear.

Based on the verdict, the sentencing guidelines for my two felony counts called for eleven and half to thirteen years in prison. The prosecution recommended the minimum, eleven and a half years, plus $759,000 in restitution. Even that felt like a life sentence. During those dark twelve weeks, I truly believed my life was over.

A few weeks later, I met with a federal probation officer assigned to write my Pre-Sentencing Report (PSR). A PSR, a legal document prepared by a probation officer, summarizes the social and legal background of a person convicted of a crime. The PSR is submitted to assist the court in making a decision for sentencing the defendant. The interview, which lasted about an hour, covered my background, education, family, military service, and any history of substance abuse or criminal conduct. I thought the meeting went smoothly. One detail, however, remains in my memory; the probation officer, a woman, arrived at the MCC in a very short skirt that would not be authorized for any other visitor or staff member. Her attire was completely unprofessional, a very low standard for a government official in a prison setting.

Several weeks later, when my attorney received the draft PSR, we were stunned: it contained multiple errors, including claims that I was a habitual cocaine user and had been involved in a terrorist threat. Neither was true. I had seen cocaine only once in my life—at a college party and I asked the users to leave. I had never been involved in any terrorist activity. Kevin filed a formal rebuttal to correct these falsehoods. The PSR also denied a downward departure for my military service. In a downward departure, the judge imposes a sentence below the minimum recommended by the Federal Sentencing Guidelines, based on mitigating factors, including military service, that are not sufficiently considered by the guidelines themselves. The rationale in the PSR for denying my downward departure was that I "had not lost a limb in combat." Kevin and I found that both heartless and absurd. Reading the report felt like reading about someone else entirely.

The probation officer was also responsible for verifying the government's restitution claims. Kevin provided documentation and photographs showing that many of the allegedly missing items had in fact been delivered and were in use by Navy civilian personnel. We estimated actual losses at roughly $200,000, but the probation officer simply accepted the government's original $759,000 figure—an estimate I had provided years earlier when first cooperating. Through my later research, I discovered that about $500,000 worth of materials were indeed delivered and used in aircraft hangars. Despite this evidence, which included pictures of the items being used at the naval aircraft repair facility, the findings were never revised. This lack of review, unfortunately, is all too common in the federal system.

Sentencing and Mercy

Jesus spent only a brief time in custody before being sentenced for his alleged crime of blasphemy. That short time was horrific. He was beaten and tortured by Roman soldiers.

He stood before the Roman governor, Pontius Pilate, to be judged for crimes he did not commit. As his Passion unfolded, even his closest friends, including Peter, abandoned him. I can only imagine the sorrow, loneliness, and humiliation the innocent Jesus felt as he stood before his earthly judge. He endured it all out of obedience to his Father and love for us.

As I was led into the courtroom on a Monday morning in May 2013, I was granted a small window into Jesus' Passion, an experience that has shaped every day of my life since. I shared—however imperfectly—in that humiliation. The courtroom was full—more than seventy people in attendance—as U.S. Marshals escorted me to my seat. Like Jesus, I saw my mother witnessing the entire proceeding. Unlike Jesus, I was surrounded by family, friends, and colleagues who came to support Colette and me. I had asked that our children not attend. My shame and sorrow were unbearable, yet God gave me the grace to remain present. I fully expected to receive a sentence of at least seven or eight years in prison—and that was my most optimistic outlook.

I hadn't planned to speak. Anger simmered within me, and I struggled to contain it. I quietly sobbed throughout much of the hearing until one of the Marshals warned me to compose myself or be removed from the courtroom. If you could paint a picture of a man stripped of all dignity, it would have been me that morning. I later learned that several parishioners from my church had gathered outside the courthouse, praying the rosary for me and for Judge Burns.

Many people, even those of faith, struggle to believe in miracles. Yet I have witnessed a few in my life, and on May 20, 2013, I received one, God's grace expressed through the mercy of a federal judge not known for leniency. In the U.S. justice system, defendants who choose to go to trial and are found guilty are typically punished more harshly than those who accept plea deals. This practice seems contrary to justice, but it is the reality. Perhaps Judge Burns was moved by the letters written on my behalf and by the full courtroom of supporters. Even the jury box was filled with people there for me. Unless you've stood before another human being who has the power to take away your freedom for a decade or more, it's hard to grasp the weight of that moment. As I stood before Judge Burns, anger, defiance, shame, sorrow, and guilt were all colliding inside me.

The judge was known for fairness but also for being stern, especially toward defendants who showed little remorse. The prosecutors, as expected, recommended eleven and a half years in prison and argued against any leniency for military service. Kevin, my attorney, countered with a request for probation, arguing that I was not a threat to the community, was unlikely to reoffend, and had served my country faithfully for twenty years, including four combat deployments. To my astonishment, Judge Burns agreed. He rejected the government's request for a long sentence, acknowledged my service, and expressed his belief that I would never reoffend. Then he invited me to speak, saying that I owed an explanation to all those who had come to support me, or at least, that's how I heard it.

I spoke. I accepted responsibility and asked for forgiveness. Judge Burns responded with compassion, reminding everyone of the value of military service and recognizing that I had led a meaningful, honorable life. Then he pronounced my sentence: thirty-six months in prison, with restitution of $759,000 to be paid jointly with my co-defendants.

I was stunned. Escorted back to the Metropolitan Correctional Center through the underground tunnel, I told other inmates that I had received only three years. They couldn't believe it—a 75 percent reduction despite going to trial. Some assumed I must have cooperated with the government. I hadn't. I believe Judge Burns had simply cooperated with grace. That day, I didn't receive just a reduced sentence, I received mercy and the chance to rebuild my life in a timeframe that wouldn't destroy my family. It took time for me to grasp the magnitude of that gift, but that day marked the beginning of my healing. My wounds and shame eventually became the source of my strength, allowing me to serve others today.

Colette understood the grace of that moment immediately. She wept, not from sorrow, but from relief. Thirty-six months in federal prison meant about thirty-one months with good behavior. I would also be eligible for up to six months in a halfway house or home confinement. Having already spent three months in custody, I would likely be away from home for just two more years. Colette knew she could endure that, and her strength helped me begin to do the same.

An Alternative to Punitive Justice

In the United States, crime is broadly defined as any act that violates the law. Running a red light, stealing groceries, or embezzling from an employer—all are crimes, regardless of motive or need. The American justice system is retributive by design: it focuses on punishment, often through lengthy incarceration, as the primary response to wrongdoing.

In the chapters that follow, I explore an alternative approach—restorative justice—a model that aligns more closely with the justice Jesus calls us to live. Restorative justice seeks not only accountability but also healing. Rather than asking, what law was broken and how we should punish, restorative justice asks what harm was done, who was affected, and how can we make it right?

Jesus' justice restores right relationships, with God, with others, and within ourselves. It is the justice of mercy, reconciliation, and truth. Restorative justice reflects this divine model. It mirrors the justice God extended again and again to his chosen people, the Israelites, offering correction, yes, but always for the sake of renewal and relationship. Jesus and his Father are justice—real, permanent justice. Jesus perfects justice through his mercy and forgiveness, and when we ask the Father for mercy and justice we can always go to Jesus as the great mediator. Our secular model of justice is inadequate because too often it does not include mercy and forgiveness, and it eliminates the possibility for reconciliation and restoration of relationships. With Jesus' justice, the goal is always reconciliation and restoring right relationships with God and each other. Jesus' justice requires patience, forgiveness, mercy, and an abundance of love. Jesus' justice includes accountability and sometimes punishment, but both accountability and punishment serve as tools to bring us back in right relationship with God and each other. Jesus' justice, perfected by his sacrifice on the cross, provides all of us with the opportunity for salvation and eternal life.

When I entered prison, I had never heard the term "restorative justice." I first encountered it about six months before my release. Since then, I have come to see it as the very heart of the Gospel's message about justice. The following chapters will examine our moral obligations toward those who are incarcerated and the essential work of helping returning citizens reintegrate into society with dignity and hope.

Restorative justice emphasizes the harm caused by crime and focuses on repairing that harm. Contrary to the voices of many critics, it is not a "soft" approach to crime. Serious sanctions, including incarceration, may still be appropriate within a restorative framework. The difference is that accountability is coupled with empathy, and punishment serves the goal of restoration rather than vengeance. Within the U.S. retributive model, victims rarely have a meaningful role in shaping charges, punishment, or reparations. In a restorative system, by contrast, the victim—not the offender—is the central figure. The victim's voice and needs guide the process of accountability and restitution.

The chapters ahead will outline restorative approaches that can be applied across the criminal justice continuum—from law enforcement and prosecution to corrections and reentry. When society invests in the restoration of its most vulnerable and marginalized members, everyone benefits. Restorative justice gives victims, offenders, and communities the opportunity to heal, thrive, and grow. As you continue reading, I hope that you will gain a deeper understanding of how restorative justice transforms not only systems but also souls, and why our current punitive approach fails to meet the needs of victims, offenders, and society alike.

Chapter 5

Visiting the Prisoner

A Call to Charity

The Catholic faith teaches that the three theological virtues—faith, hope, and love, also known as charity—are joined with the four cardinal virtues of justice, prudence, temperance, and courage, discussed earlier in Chapter 3. These virtues guide us on our pilgrim journey toward holiness and unity with the Father, Son, and Holy Spirit. In his First Letter to the Corinthians, St. Paul identifies love, or charity, as the greatest of the theological virtues. God is love, and we most fully abide in him when we love both God and one another. Catholics embrace charity as an act that draws them, and all people, closer to God and all humanity.

In Matthew's Gospel, Jesus reminds his listeners of their duty to one another as an expression of our love for God:

> [Jesus said] "Then the King will say to those on his right hand, 'Come, you that are blessed by my Father, inherit the kingdom prepared for you from the foundation of the world; for I was hungry and you gave me food, I was thirsty and you gave me something to drink, I was a stranger and you welcomed me, I was naked and you gave me clothing, I was sick and you took care of me, I was in prison and you visited me.'

> Then the righteous will answer him, 'Lord, when was it we saw you hungry and gave you food, or thirsty and gave you something to drink? And when was it that we saw you a stranger and welcomed you, or naked and gave you clothing? And when was it that we saw you sick or in prison and visited you?' And the king will answer them, 'Truly I tell you, just as you did it to one of the least of these who are members of my family, you did it to me.' Then he will say to those at his left hand, 'You that are accursed, depart from me into the eternal fire prepared for the devil and his angels, for I was hungry and you gave me no food, I was thirsty and you gave me nothing to drink, I was a stranger and you did not welcome me, naked and you did not give me clothing, sick and in prison and you did not visit me.' Then they also will answer, 'Lord, when was it we saw you hungry or thirsty or a stranger or naked or sick or in prison, and did not take care of you?' Then he will answer them, 'Truly I tell you, just as you did not do it to one of the least of these, you did not do it to me.'" (Mt 25:34–45)

The people of God are called to live Matthew 25 to the best of their ability and capacity. This gospel passage identifies the seven-corporal works of mercy: feeding the hungry, giving drink to the thirsty, clothing the naked, visiting the sick, sheltering the homeless, visiting the imprisoned, and burying the dead. These works meet the physical needs of the poor and marginalized, including immigrants and prisoners. Christians are obliged to undertake these works of mercy in order to provide for the material needs of the poor and needy living on the margins of society. Practicing them is a reminder that we are all God's children and that Christian faith, rooted in the Gospel, demands preferential care for the poor and vulnerable.

Among these works of mercy, the most neglected is visiting the prisoner. Prisoners are often among society's most marginalized. Before incarceration most inmates have experienced food insecurity, homelessness, substance abuse, and physical or sexual trauma. Most were already living on society's margins and, tragically, after release return to those same conditions. A prison visit is an act of love toward the inmate and toward God. It acknowledges that the prisoner exists and matters. Regular contact with family and friends greatly improves an inmate's mental health and reintegration success upon release.

Correctional staff and even inmates themselves often do not recognize a prisoner's human dignity. A visit from a loved one, friend, or community member loudly proclaims that an inmate still matters and deserves dignity. For a moment, that visit erases his invisibility and shame. God calls Christians to visit the prisoner because he wants them to love even those who have sinned and harmed others. Loving the prisoner can be difficult, even painful, yet God still commands it. Family and close friends have a special responsibility to visit their loved ones in prison, yet the travel costs and logistical challenges can be overwhelming. Most prisons in the United States are in rural areas, far from major cities, making visits costly and time-consuming. Today, however, phone calls, email, and even video visitation offer ways to maintain contact. Studies show that inmates who maintain regular communication with loved ones have significantly higher chances of successful reintegration.

While not everyone can physically visit the imprisoned, all can pray for them. The cost of travel can make visits impossible, especially for the poor, but prayer knows no boundaries. "Visiting the prisoner" can mean writing letters or emails. Many nonprofit and religious organizations sponsor pen-pal programs for the incarcerated, powerful acts of charity that affirm dignity and hope. Visiting the prisoner can also mean reaching out to their families, who often suffer silently. God wants his creatures, even in our modern time, to keep the prisoner and his family in their prayers, and when possible, visit them and the families who are left behind.

Christian faith supports two complementary truths: compassion for the incarcerated and dignity for victims of crime. Christians support the dignity of victims of crime, and they demand accountability for those that have committed crime. Visiting the prisoner does not condone wrongdoing; it proclaims that every person, even one who has sinned, retains God-given dignity. When the rehabilitated return, the faith community must welcome them home.

Dropping Into the Belly of the Beast

The prophet Jonah initially fled from God's call to deliver a message to the people of Nineveh. His disobedience led to misfortune, culminating in him being thrown into the sea and swallowed by a great fish—literally into "the belly of the beast." Today, the phrase "belly of the beast" describes any dangerous or uncertain situation. It's no surprise, then, that prison is often called by that name. It is a world apart—isolated, unpredictable, and often dangerous, both from fellow inmates and, at times, from correctional staff.

Prisoners in the United States live in a perpetual state of uncertainty. A single act of violence or a health crisis can lock down an entire facility for days or even weeks. During lockdowns, visits stop completely, and inmates lose contact with family, volunteers, and religious or educational programs. These periods are the most isolating times for the incarcerated. The prisoner lives in the belly of the beast with a constant sense of insecurity, both physical and psychological. Visits from loved ones provide a measure of certainty that serve many purposes, most notably that they still matter to someone from the outside world. Particularly, those who receive regular visits from loved ones are far more likely upon release to succeed in reentering society.

While incarcerated, I was blessed to receive frequent visits from family and friends. During my initial confinement at the MCC in San Diego, my wife, parents, and children visited me regularly since the facility was only fifteen minutes from our home. Many federal prisons restrict visitation through a points system. MCC San Diego was no exception, but I was allowed to receive about one visit a week. Visits in detention centers or jails are typically "no-contact," meaning you cannot hug or shake hands with your visitor—something that can make even a brief meeting emotionally difficult.

The visits I received while awaiting sentencing were among the hardest. I lived in a haze of anxiety, uncertain whether my sentence would be five, ten, or thirteen years. My family shared my fear, yet they still endured the weekly security checks to see me. Each visit began and ended with a full-body search by correctional officers, an invasive and humiliating procedure that strips away any sense of dignity. Though such searches may be justified for security reasons, all the same they are degrading.

Most people will never experience incarceration, but family and friends who visit loved ones behind bars enter that world, if only for a short time. The experience can be unsettling. Visitors can be denied entry for arbitrary reasons—wrong-colored clothing, inappropriate shoes, or an officer's subjective judgment. My eighty-five-year-old mother was once turned away because her slacks were deemed too similar in color to inmate uniforms. She was devastated and humiliated. Sadly, it is common for correctional staff to treat visitors with the same condescension and lack of respect that they show inmates. It should concern everyone greatly that a public employee feels free to disrespect citizens simply because they have a family member in prison or jail.

36434-298

The first man in Scripture had a name: Adam. Since creation, every human being has been given a name, a mark of personhood and belonging. In our culture, names identify who we are and what family we belong: our name is our identity. In prison, however, that name becomes a number. Correctional staff refer to inmates primarily by their assigned number. When you are called for a work detail, meeting, or visit, it is not by name but by number. This practice, while administrative, has deep psychological consequences. In God's kingdom, names confer meaning and dignity. Scripture itself affirms this through genealogies—Adam to Abraham, David to Jesus—reminding us that names locate us within God's story. Losing your name, even temporarily, feels like losing part of your humanity.

In the military, it's common to address others by rank and last name, a custom that still conveys respect. During my service, I always made an effort to address others properly—by rank and name if senior or junior, or first name if a peer. In prison, there is no such courtesy. Your first and last name are reduced to a number. The Nazis amplified this form of dehumanization by tattooing prisoner numbers on concentration camp inmates. Sadly, some incarcerated individuals in the U.S. adopt this same practice, tattooing their prison numbers on their bodies. I knew a man from Los Angeles who had tattooed on the back of his head "112"—the last three digits of his Bureau of Prisons number, signifying the Los Angeles district.

I always dreaded hearing my number, except when it meant I had a visitor. Then, it didn't matter what they called me. My number is 36434-298. I refer to it in the present tense because I will always carry it. If I were ever re-incarcerated, I would again become 36434-298. The last three digits, 298, mark that my offense was committed in San Diego. While in federal prison in Colorado, that code set me apart among inmates mostly from the intermountain West—Colorado, Montana, New Mexico, Utah, and Idaho.

Most federal prisons operate on a points system, limiting the number and duration of visits each month. The Federal Prison Camp in Florence, however, had no such restriction, allowing unlimited visits. I was fortunate to have that possibility and blessed to receive one or two visits each month.

In mid-June 2013 I was transferred from Oklahoma City to Federal Prison Camp, Florence. During that transition, I had not been able to speak with my wife. When I finally called her from Colorado, I asked her to send visitor clearance forms to family and friends who wanted to visit. Every visitor must be approved by the Bureau of Prisons, a process that takes several weeks. Florence is 1,500 miles from my home in San Diego, so all visits required advance planning for airline tickets, lodging, and a rental car. Florence is about an hour south of Colorado Springs and two hours from Denver International Airport, making visits difficult and costly. My first visitor was one of my closest friends and mentors from the Marine Corps, Mike Linehan. While he and his wife were traveling cross-country in their RV they happened to pass through Colorado. Mike wrote to my counselor requesting permission to visit me, and miraculously, the counselor expedited his approval.

Mike is a bit of a legend in U.S. Marine aviation. He began his Marine Corps career as an enlisted man, rising through the ranks to become an officer. Known affectionately as "The Godfather," Mike was respected by everyone—from generals to young enlisted Marines. Since the 1990s, when we first met, his leadership and compassion profoundly influenced me. That he became my first visitor was no coincidence—it was a "God-incidence," gift from God.

In the visiting room, Mike bought me my first vending machine meal, a cheeseburger and a Coke. He visited Friday evening and again on Saturday, sharing stories from our Marine days and his own youthful missteps. His message was simple: "It's going to be okay. There is life after prison." His visit brought the consolation and hope I sorely needed. I needed to hear those words from him. I never worked directly for Mike, but our relationship was such that I never wanted to disappoint him. At that point I felt I had disappointed everyone. But Mike reminded me that true friendship endures through failure, and he would still be my friend when I returned home. His visit restored my sense of worth and gave me hope for life beyond prison. I have been richly blessed with Mike's friendship and loyalty for more than thirty years.

When Mike's wife, Marylyn, passed away from pancreatic cancer in 2020, her death drew us even closer. Mike stood by me when I was at my lowest, and we remain committed to one another. I have been walking with him on his own faith journey as a widower, and I am happy to write that he has returned to his faith full of love for God and our Church.

Prison Camp Sanctuary

During the two years I was at Florence, Colette visited me twenty-six times. Equally, if not more intensely, she felt the trauma I endured before and during my incarceration.

My trial and sentencing were reported in the local paper, and the small community where we lived across the bay from San Diego was quick to gossip. Colette had to endure whispers—and sometimes direct questions—about why she would remain with her "convicted felon" husband.

Before prison I thought I knew my wife. We had already weathered my thirteen-month deployment to Iraq and many challenges at home. Yet through this ordeal I came to understand her more deeply. Colette was extraordinary, the heroine for me and our children. While I was incarcerated, her ex-husband sought full custody of her children, arguing she was unfit because of my imprisonment. She worked full-time as an eye surgeon at Kaiser Permanente, managed dwindling finances after legal fees, and raised four children largely on her own. During this period of our life Colette was a super-human, wonder woman. Despite all the life challenges, for those two years she visited me at least one weekend every month.

When Colette and I were dating, she told me that there are two ways to experience unconditional love when young: through one's parents and through God's Church. Not everyone receives both, but as a young person I was blessed with both, and as an adult with a third, Colette's steadfast love. Even when I felt unworthy, her faith in God, our family, and in me helped me heal and learn to love myself again. It took years, but her love rekindled my love for God, myself, and others.

Visiting hours began Friday evenings and continued through Saturday and Sunday, including holidays such as Christmas and New Year's Day. Each weekend offered up to seventeen visiting hours, three on Friday evening and seven each on Saturday and Sunday. On Friday morning Colette would fly from San Diego to Denver, drive two hours to Florence, check into the modest Super 8 Motel near the prison, and arrive in time for the evening visit. Those weekends we would spend nearly every available hour together. During the rest of each month, I counted down the days until I could see her again.

Even amid hardship, blessings can be found. Though we were far from happy with our circumstances, we found joy in simply being together. How many couples get to spend seventeen uninterrupted hours in conversation during a weekend? In the visiting room, there were no phones, no TV, no distractions—only board games, vending machines, and time to talk. We talked about everything: our children, our families, our dreams for the future. I sometimes fantasized about moving abroad and starting a new life. Colette just listened—never dismissing my impractical ideas, only offering presence and love.

Colette modeled God's love as only a devoted spouse can. Scripture describes the relationship between Christ and the Church as that of bridegroom and bride; through her I experienced that divine reflection. There were times when I felt so angry that I would try to push her away, telling her that life would be easier without me. During many of our phone conversations I was mean and harsh. Colette's response mirrored how God responds to the wounded, with love and compassion. Even when I was at my worst, she continued to love me unconditionally, just as God loves us despite our flaws. At those moments, my wounds and shame made it hard to return her love, but she never wavered. Like all of us, she may not be perfect, yet she is perfect for me—steadfast in faith and love.

Twice a year Colette also brought our four children to visit. The cost—over $2,000 for airfare, car rental, and lodging—was a heavy burden, but she made it happen. Such financial barriers prevent many incarcerated parents from seeing their children. Studies show that maintaining contact during incarceration benefits both parent and child, strengthening emotional and psychological wellbeing. After Colette brought the kids to visit for my first Christmas in prison, she even took them skiing for a few days to create happy memories despite our pain.

In addition to Colette's visits, I am deeply grateful for the love and support of many family members who came to see me. During my first summer in Florence my parents drove from Park City, Utah, sharing stories of the fourteen-thousand-foot mountain peaks they passed along the way. Throughout my imprisonment, they continued to provide steady support for Colette and our children. Later that year, another visit by my parents, brother, and sister-in-law was canceled after a violent incident on the prison yard. They were heartbroken but made the best of the trip by exploring Denver and touring the Coors Brewery, my father and brother's favorite beer.

My brother Rich has always been my best friend. Though we've had different life experiences, I respect him more than anyone else. Shortly after my sentencing hearing, he visited me at the MCC San Diego. He encouraged me to accept my three-year sentence rather than appeal, wisely reminding me that prolonging the legal battle would only burden Colette and our family further. His advice opened the road to healing. In the summer of 2014 he visited me again, this time with his wife, Patty, in Florence. My sister-in-law gently told me how important it was for Rich to see me and visit with me. I began to realize that visits were not only a source of strength for me, but also a source of comfort and healing for my loved ones. During my incarceration Rich would write me often, always signing off with "love and prayers, Rich."

My cousin Fred and his wife Autumn, who I consider more like a brother and sister, spent a weekend visiting me. They live in Northern California, but the rest of our family live on the East Coast, so they and those of us from Southern California refer to ourselves as the West Coast Ehnows. Living far from our Philadelphia family, Fred and I had grown especially close over the years.

Others also made the long journey to visit—college friends from New York, neighbors from San Diego, even my former commanding officer, Colonel Guy Close, who came with Bart Steidl, another fellow squadron commander from my days in Iraq. Their loyalty reflects the Marine Corps motto *Semper Fidelis*—"Always Faithful." Without judging me, my neighbor Jeff Pace, a San Diego police officer, visited and introduced me to the concept of restorative justice, assuring me that God still had a plan for my life. Neighbors that lived across the street from us, JJ and Sveta Gentry, made the trek to spend a weekend with me. I was truly blessed with the many friends that travelled far and wide to visit.

My pastor, Father Mike Murphy, visited me at MCC San Diego and twice in Colorado. During his first visit at the prison camp, he even brought the Eucharist, allowing me the indescribable grace of receiving Christ's presence. Father Mike, who also serves as Colette's spiritual director, never judged me. He embodies what Catholics mean when they say a priest acts *in persona Christi*—in the person of Christ. The visits from my family, friends, and pastor sustained me. They reminded me that I still mattered—to those I loved and to God. These encounters were essential for my healing and prepared me to reintegrate into society after release.

Sadly, though such visits play an invaluable role in sustaining the faith of inmates and easing their transition back into parish life, few clergy regularly visit those behind bars. I believe more priests and deacons are called to this ministry of presence, to bring light into one of the darkest corners of our world. Later chapters will touch on the clergy's role in supporting an inmate's reintegration back into parish life.

A World within the Prison World

The visiting room in a prison is a world within a world—a rare place where amid despair joy can briefly exist. It is sometimes the only space where inmates and their loved ones can feel human again. Colette was considered a "regular" in the visiting room since she came at least once a month. Over time, she formed friendships with other wives who also visited regularly. They would often coordinate their trips, spend time together after visiting hours, share meals, and through shared pain comfort one another. Most of these women were married to white-collar offenders who, like us, had the means to visit frequently.

Colette always stayed about half a mile from the prison at the Super 8 Motel. The owners, compassionate folks from Colorado, became part of her support system. The man, a retired deputy sheriff, showed genuine empathy for families of the incarcerated. On holidays like Valentine's Day, Easter, and Christmas, he and his partner placed flowers, chocolates, or cards in the rooms of women visiting loved ones. When they eventually married, they even invited Colette to the wedding. In their own quiet way, they lived out the message of Matthew 25: serving Christ through acts of mercy and kindness.

At Florence, my calendar revolved around anticipated visits. I kept one prison uniform reserved solely for visitation days, much like a Marine keeps a dress uniform ready for inspection. I made sure it was freshly washed, neatly pressed, and spotless. Before every visit, I showered and groomed carefully. Visiting days weren't just important, they were sacred. They felt almost as meaningful as receiving the Eucharist. In fact, the visitors were the living Eucharist for me as the face of Christ in them was fully present with me during the visits. Visits gave us what every prisoner desperately needs—hope. Hope sustains faith and makes charity possible. When the camp was locked down due to violence or a health outbreak, and visits were suspended, a heavy gloom settled over everyone.

Out of more than six hundred inmates at the prison camp, only about fifty received regular visits. Most men considered themselves fortunate if they saw family once or twice a year. Some had gone more than a decade without a single visitor. The absence of contact with the outside world is both devastating and deeply contrary to rehabilitation. People of faith—and all people of goodwill—must remember prisoners in prayer and in action, whether through letters, visits, or advocacy for laws that protect their dignity. For those who live the Christian faith, the corporal acts of mercy, especially visiting the sick and the prisoner, are not luxuries; rather, they are obligations.

Visits provide the incarcerated a powerful morale boost, reminding them that they are still seen, known, and loved. Research consistently shows that after release, inmates who have maintained family and community connections have lower recidivism rates and better outcomes.

These first five chapters have focused on the front and middle stages of the criminal justice system: the prosecution of crimes, the courts, and the correctional system. I offer my experiences to illuminate the reality of that world. The next chapters will provide insight into what happens after release, how the formerly incarcerated can rebuild their lives and what our faith and communities can do to support their reintegration. Part 2 of this book moves from inside the system back to the outside world.

Part II

Outside

"As I walked out the door toward the gate that would lead to my freedom, I knew if I didn't leave my bitterness and hatred behind, I'd still be in prison."

—Nelson Mandela

Chapter 6

Welcoming Home

Reintegration

During my military career, I was deployed overseas in combat zones several times. Unlike Vietnam-era veterans, who were often ridiculed and unappreciated upon their return, my homecomings were always positive and commemorative. Since the end of the Vietnam War in the 1970s, our society has collectively supported and welcomed returning service members. Honoring our veterans remains a bipartisan cause; most citizens, regardless of political affiliation, agree that returning military personnel should be welcomed and appreciated.

In contrast, prisoners returning to their communities typically come home without fanfare or recognition. While a military member may receive a hero's welcome, a returning prisoner is often ignored. Such a welcome may not be appropriate, but some form of acknowledgment can help to begin the process of reintegration into family and community life. This chapter explores the essential elements that a returning citizen needs to successfully rejoin society. My own reintegration was marked by support, compassion, and success—an exception to what most returning citizens experience.

Reintegration is not mere reentry. Every person released from jail or prison experiences reentry, the act of physically returning to society. Reintegration, however, implies successful restoration into communities of belonging—family, professional, and spiritual. Beyond release, it signifies assimilation and renewal. Only a minority of those who complete their sentence and return achieve reintegration. Reintegration reflects God's call to help others rebuild their lives—and because it's beneficial for returning citizens to be good neighbors, parents, and friends that in turn make stronger communities.

Each year, the more than six hundred thousand men and women released from jail or prison are expected to reintegrate into society. Most, lacking the necessary economic and social resources to succeed, require substantial support. Five elements are essential for reintegration: employment, housing, access to health care, family support and connections, and when needed substance abuse treatment.

Stability rests upon these five pillars—not only for returning citizens but for all who wish to thrive. These essentials can be taken for granted, but former prisoners often have never experienced such stability. The most critical, employment, sustains the other elements. A job provides income for housing, access to healthcare, and resources for counseling or treatment. Family support may offer financial help, but also reinforces a sense of worth and belonging through emotional affirmation.

Social capital—a network of personal and professional relationships—is also crucial to success. Those with strong social capital may find jobs and opportunities more easily. Those who become incarcerated, however, may have little or no social capital before entering the system, and with time in prison it diminishes further. Reintegration is a kind of rebirth: full of potential yet limited by inexperience and lack of support. During my own reintegration, though ultimately successful, I faced many challenges. In this chapter, I will share my journey and the experiences of others I've encountered across San Diego and Southern California in my ministry for returning citizens.

Finally, I will highlight the role each member of the Body of Christ can play in welcoming returning men and women into their communities and parishes. Spiritual support—rarely mentioned in discussions of reintegration—is, in fact, essential. My own research and experience suggest, an additional component of reintegration not usually included in the research and best practices regarding successful prisoner reintegration—spiritual care. The love and acceptance of my faith community made my own reintegration possible. Although social science research on prisoner reentry often overlooks the importance of the spiritual dimension, I have come to believe that lasting reintegration also depends on spiritual support.

Resurrection

Jesus was crucified on a Friday. To his followers, the crucifixion appeared to be the tragic end of the man they loved and believed to be the Son of God—the Messiah. They thought all hope was lost. Yet Christian faith, based on more than five hundred eyewitness accounts recorded by the Gospel writers and the Apostle Paul makes clear that the crucifixion was not the end but the beginning. What seemed final on that dark day became, through God's mystery, the most significant event in human history: the Resurrection of Jesus Christ. His death was necessary for the sanctification of humankind; his Resurrection is the foundation of the Christian faith.

Jesus' story is the story of God's incarnation—love made flesh. Each of us experiences moments that mirror, in small ways, the passion and hope of Christ. In my own way, I came to understand a fraction of his suffering and sacrifice during what I call my "small passion." Though my trials were insignificant compared to those of Jesus, during my tribulation I remained hopeful that God would lead me to restoration—a personal resurrection.

At times, our lives echo Jesus' earthly journey. We endure pain, betrayal, or loss that becomes the catalyst for new life and deeper faith. My own "passion" was my trial and incarceration—a time of suffering and despair for me and my family. My restoration began when I was released from prison. Jesus promised to "rebuild the temple in three days," and three days after his death he did rebuild his temple, his body, in a resurrected state. My resurrection took much longer—closer to three years—and was marked by setbacks and many challenges.

After nearly twenty-seven months in custody, on May 20, 2015, I left Florence, Colorado. Until October 13, when my sentence ended, I would remain in custody under the Bureau of Prisons, first at a halfway house in San Diego and then on home confinement. The Bureau gave me a Greyhound bus ticket from Pueblo, Colorado, to San Diego—the only travel method permitted. Colette, my heroine, met me at the bus station in Pueblo, and we began the twenty-four-hour trip home together. I don't think I let go of her hand the entire journey. I wasn't free yet, but I was getting closer.

As I left Florence, I already had the four essential elements for reintegration: housing, employment, family connections, and access to health care. I knew how blessed I was to have these elements coupled with the unwavering love of family and friends.

My first moment of true restoration came when I attended Mass at my home parish in Coronado, Sacred Heart on May 24, 2015, Pentecost Sunday. My pastor, Father Mike Murphy, had written to the halfway house administrator requesting permission for me to attend. As Colette and I drove to church that morning, conflicting emotions of shame and relief overwhelmed me—shame for my past yet hope for renewal. We sat in our usual pew with my parents. I remember little about the liturgy itself, but I will never forget receiving the Eucharist at my home parish for the first time in over two years.

As I proceeded to receive Communion, Father Mike placed the Eucharist in my hand, then set down the ciborium, embraced me, and said simply, "Welcome home." In that moment, the love of my pastor and my Church lifted away my shame. Acting in persona Christi, he welcomed me as the father welcomed the prodigal son. His words—"Welcome home"—marked a turning point. His embrace told me that I still mattered and had a place in the Body of Christ. Though challenges lay ahead, that hopeful moment of acceptance set me on a path toward healing and wholeness. I did not return in a resurrected body as Jesus did, yet returning on Pentecost Sunday to my faith community marked the beginning of my spiritual and emotional resurrection.

Being welcomed back into my parish community was the ideal, one that I wish was the norm. Every returning citizen deserves that kind of welcome—a sign from their community that they are still loved, still valued, and still capable of living a life with purpose.

Transitional Housing and Home Confinement

Although I had the essential elements for successful reintegration—housing, employment, family, and health care—my reentry proved to be the most difficult part of my experience with the corrections and criminal justice system. I recall these events with a certain level of anger and indignation. What follows is a candid recollection of that period—one that exposed deep flaws in the programs meant to support returning citizens.

The Bureau of Prisons (BOP) typically releases inmates to transitional housing facilities when about six months remain on their sentence. The time spent there depends on factors such as housing availability, family support, and the nature of the offense. Transitional housing—often called community reentry or halfway housing—allows the BOP to maintain custody while an individual lives in the community. For the last five months of my sentence, I lived in such a facility coupled with supervised home confinement.

In California, many federal and state reentry facilities are privately owned and operated by for-profit corporations that also manage private prisons. These companies profit by warehousing human beings, and exercising powers, in my opinion, that should belong solely to the government. Nationwide, more than one hundred and fifty private prisons and countless reentry centers are run by companies like CoreCivic, Management & Training Corporation, and the GEO Group. These corporations, which lobby aggressively in Washington and state capitals, employ thousands and generate billions in revenue. In my experience and research, their profit motives often undermine transparency and rehabilitation, revealing the dangers of outsourcing such a profound government responsibility.

I was first assigned to a reentry center on Boston Avenue near the San Diego Naval Base. After my wife and parents dropped me off, things quickly got complicated. Because some of my codefendants had testified against me, I was barred from being housed with them. Yet, when I arrived one of those very codefendants—the ringleader of the fraud scheme—was at the facility. I immediately told the desk counselor, "We have a problem." Pointing to my former codefendant, I said, "That man is a snitch! That man testified against me; we can't be housed together."

Looking back, I realize how easily I had adopted the inmate code—the unwritten rules of "honor" that condemn cooperating witnesses, known in prison slang as snitches. I had refused to testify against others, believing I was doing the honorable thing. My co-defendant, who had harmed so many and bilked the government out of millions, after testifying for the government received nearly the same sentence as I did. My sense of injustice seethed in me deeply. Though time has softened my anger, I continue to pray for healing and the ability for true forgiveness for those that testified against me.

After waiting for about nine hours, I was reassigned to another facility two miles away—a much larger center housing around 550 people from federal, state, and county systems. It was operated by CoreCivic, one of the leading for-profit prison companies. The place was filthy and chaotic, the worst possible environment for someone seeking a smooth transition back into society. I was assigned to an eight-man bunk room in a federal unit that held ninety-six men. Only one toilet worked; the others were clogged or broken. In the outdoor areas, drug use and even public sexual activity were common. The conditions were dehumanizing—a stark contrast to the relative order and cleanliness of federal prison life, where inmates typically maintained mutual respect and basic hygiene.

I stayed at the transitional housing facility for about thirty days, until I was reassigned to home confinement. Thankfully, I began working immediately. My friend and employer scheduled me for long shifts six days a week, allowing me to spend as little time at the facility as possible. CoreCivic held contracts with the BOP, the California

Department of Corrections and Rehabilitation, and San Diego County Probation—contracts worth millions. On top of this, the company took twenty-five percent of every resident's wages. The entire setup was exploitative—a system profiting from human suffering under the guise of rehabilitation. CoreCivic earns over two billion dollars annually, yet in my experience provides little of true value to the people it houses.

Over the past decade, in my ministry work I have continued visiting that same facility, and conditions have changed little. Some they say have worsened. Residents report that staff intentionally delay home confinement placements to retain more people (and thus more revenue). After I was finally allowed to transition to home confinement, I still had to report weekly for drug testing at the CoreCivic facility which was also responsible for supervising my home confinement.

We were required to install a landline so the facility could monitor me. They called daily between ten at night and six in the morning, and I had to submit a weekly schedule for approval. I was permitted to work, attend church, shop for necessities, and exercise—but nothing more. Occasionally, counselors would check on me at home or at work, though these visits eventually stopped once they saw I was complying with my weekly schedule. Despite my negative opinion of the CoreCivic facility and their operating procedures, including the collection of a portion of inmates' wages, the counselors and most of the work staff were professional and supportive of me and others who were reentering.

When I returned home, I had been away from Colette and the children for more than two years. She had become accustomed to life as a single parent, and my two teenaged stepchildren were asserting their independence. I naïvely believed everything would return to normal once I came home, but I encountered resentment and tension. Our oldest children, Brendan, and Caitilin, were away at college while I was incarcerated, and so were somewhat insulated from the family dynamics of this period. My step-daughter, Kelly, estranged from her own father, was particularly wounded. My absence, heightened her worry and concern for Colette, who bore the burden of the stress and financial uncertainty caused by my incarceration. Likewise, my stepson Eric felt the effects, also with worry about me and his mom.

My parents, who lived in a cottage on our property, had been extraordinary in supporting Colette and the kids. At the time I, a returning and traumatized outsider, could not yet fully appreciate their pain, particularly Kelly's.

That first year was extraordinarily difficult for our family. But through love, faith, and the support of friends and our parish community we survived. At the same time, because lawsuits over debts from our former business began to mount, we had to file for bankruptcy to protect our home and savings. It was an exhausting period of uncertainty and financial strain. Every dollar Colette earned seemed to go to lawyers or court fees. My faith told me that God was guiding us, but that assurance didn't make the journey easier.

The halfway house and home confinement experience were profoundly negative. Rather than supporting my reintegration, the system managed by a private corporation seemed designed for profit, not people. Most residents had no assets, yet they were charged fees and given little help finding jobs, writing résumés, or preparing for interviews. The overcrowded facility served only to warehouse human beings—not to provide a bridge back to community life.

All citizens, regardless of political belief, should be alarmed that taxpayer dollars fund such ineffective and exploitative programs. My experience convinced me that CoreCivic's facility hindered rather than helped my reentry.

Given the choice, I would have preferred to serve my final five months in prison rather than endure the indignity of that system.

God's Time

Being the father of two children and two stepchildren is a blessing, yet a challenge. My trial and imprisonment only intensified the difficulties Colette and I faced in blending families and raising children from former marriages. My daughter, Caitie, was an especially spirited teenager with a big personality—eccentric, lively, and full of energy. She was seven when her mother and I divorced, and nine when I married Colette. Caitie quickly became the self-appointed leader for her stepsiblings, Kelly and Eric. She adored them, but she could also be a tyrant.

Around age fourteen, Caitie began pulling away from the family. My son, Brendan, stayed with Colette and me, but Caitie stayed with her mother. Like many teens, she prioritized her friends and found our house rules too strict. She stopped coming over regularly and refused to attend church with us. Wisely, our pastor advised us not to force her.

Spiritually and emotionally, Caitie was in crisis. She wanted nothing to do with me or Colette, and her absence broke my heart. For about six months, she refused to visit at all. Eventually, she began coming by about once a month, mainly to see Kelly and Eric. That was good enough for me—I just wanted to see her. She was still difficult and often defiant, but I loved her through it, hoping one day she'd open her heart again. It took about two years for our relationship to begin healing.

When Caitie was sixteen, we took a father-daughter trip to our townhouse near Park City, Utah. We spent the weekend hiking, listening to music, and trying to reconnect.

I told her I would always love her and always be there for her. A year later, my promise was tested when I faced the possibility of going to prison.

After graduating from high school in 2012, Caitie began community college in San Diego. When I was incarcerated in 2013, she moved to Northern California to attend the College of the Redwoods, planning to transfer to Humboldt State University. When I returned from prison in 2015, she asked to live with us for the summer—and I was thrilled. I got her a job with me at High Tide Bottle Shop and Kitchen, where we often worked the same shifts. Reconnecting with Caitie that summer was one of God's great gifts. Our prodigal daughter had returned as had the prodigal father. Caitie was more mature and joyful by this time in her life. She still had a rebellious streak—she may have inherited that from me—but she had grown into a remarkable young woman. That summer, I realized how deeply she loved me and how much my love meant to her.

One evening, while we were working together, Caitie asked if we could talk. She told me she wanted to return to the Church and receive the Sacrament of Confirmation, the third of the so-called "sacraments of initiation," together with Baptism and Holy Communion. Our other three children had been confirmed in high school, but Caitie hadn't been ready then. The same daughter who once called herself an atheist now wanted to be confirmed. Catholics believe that Confirmation seals the soul with the gifts of the Holy Spirit—and marks the confirmed in full unity with the Church. Caitie's desire to receive the sacrament was a moment of grace.

At the 2016 Easter Vigil, Caitie was confirmed at Sacred Heart Parish, Coronado. True to form, she wore a beautiful outfit paired with her signature hiking boots. Colette was her sponsor. Watching her receive that sacrament was one of the most joyful moments of my life. God had worked in his time—quietly and faithfully—to bring her home to the Church.

Many Catholic parents fear their children will drift away from the faith and perhaps never return. Statistics show that young adults between ages eighteen and thirty-nine are the least active in the Church. Catholics have much work to do to reengage them, yet they must also trust that God continues to make himself known to their children, even when they wander. Everyone experiences moments of doubt about their faith as well as about Catholic teaching. Sometimes momentarily questioning or neglecting faith can deepen it. Caitie's return to God grew out of suffering—hers, mine, and our family's. None of us seeks suffering, but it can bear spiritual fruit.

If my imprisonment helped bring my daughter back to God, I would endure it again without hesitation. Our Lord suffered and died for each of us; a little suffering on my part is nothing compared to the gift of my daughter's renewed faith. Through that experience, I glimpsed God's boundless love for each and every one of God's children.

Going Back to School

In 2012, just months before my indictment, I was accepted into the PhD program in Leadership Studies at the University of San Diego (USD). I enrolled to regain a sense of purpose amid uncertainty about my future. Once my trial was scheduled for February 2013, I requested a leave of absence from the program, unsure of what lay ahead.

While I was incarcerated, my faculty advisor, Dr. Bob Donmoyer, wrote to me periodically. His letters offered encouragement and updates, and when I was released, he urged me to reapply. I did reapply to the program from prison, and to my amazement, I was accepted back into the graduate school for the fall 2015 semester. I have always enjoyed school and learning in general, and I thought going back and earning another degree might provide a solid foundation for my reintegration. I felt blessed to have a tangible goal: to finish what I had started and an opportunity to rebuild my life through education.

The doctoral program in Leadership Studies, with a concentration in nonprofit management, is offered within the School of Leadership and Education Sciences at USD, San Diego's largest Catholic university. When I received my acceptance letter, I was overwhelmed with gratitude. The faculty had voted unanimously to readmit me, and the Department of Veterans Affairs (VA) covered my tuition in full while providing a monthly stipend and funds for books. I was being paid to pursue a doctorate—and given a second chance. My reentry plan was to complete the program and then work in the non-profit sector.

My admittance letter instructed me to meet with my faculty advisor and register for classes. While still living at the halfway house, I received permission to visit campus and meet with Dr. Donmoyer. During that meeting, I was told I would have to appear before a student conduct board because of my felony conviction. My advisor and the associate dean assured me it was a formality, but I wasn't convinced.

A few weeks later, I appeared before a three-person conduct review board composed of a graduate student, a faculty member, and an administrator. The associate dean, Ms. Linda Dews, accompanied me for support. I soon realized this was no formality. The board claimed I had violated the university's student conduct code because I had been indicted while enrolled years earlier. They presented newspaper articles as evidence and accused me of misconduct, even though my offenses occurred outside my affiliation with the university. The hearing felt like a "kangaroo court." Though I was confident and composed, I knew how it would end.

My joy in returning to school was short-lived. I was encountering my first obstacle to successful reintegration. A week after I met with the board, I received a letter expelling me from the university, with the option to reapply after three years. I was devastated—ashamed, angry, and uncertain of my future. Furious at the injustice, Colette, my pastor, and Dr. Donmoyer urged me to appeal. For a week, I wallowed in despair, convinced I would spend the rest of my life delivering pizzas. Then my frustration turned to resolve. I believed that the university had no grounds to expel me. I had not violated the student conduct code because my criminal misconduct occurred before I was associated with the university. Furthermore, I had a letter from the Graduate Admissions Council readmitting me into the program with the full knowledge that I had been incarcerated. The university's decision was wrong, and their treatment toward me was cruel.

I contacted an attorney known for successfully suing USD. Dr. Donmoyer—still a USD faculty member—accompanied me to meet the attorney. I always thought Bob Donmoyer was a man of integrity and conviction, and his accompaniment during this difficult period solidified my belief in his high character. The attorney advised me to demand reinstatement and if necessary, prepare to sue for damages. My only desire was to return to school, not to pursue litigation. The attorney sent a formal letter to the university's counsel demanding that my expulsion be overturned within fourteen days or face legal action.

Meanwhile, my pastor reached out to a friend, USD's Vice President for Ministry. Within two weeks of my attorney's letter, the university rescinded its decision. I was reinstated with two conditions: a three-year probationary period and an annual reflection paper on my rehabilitation. Though I found the stipulations demeaning, I accepted them. I had won my appeal and regained an opportunity to pursue a graduate degree at the university.

Ironically, this experience of discrimination came from a Catholic institution that publicly champions human dignity and restorative justice. The office that handled my case was even called "The Office of Ethical Development and Restorative Practices." Yet I found little restoration in how I was treated. Later, as I learned more about restorative justice, I came to realize that the university in general, and the Office of Ethical Development and Restorative Practices specifically, were not practicing the values espoused by the university and the office.

By late summer, I was finally able to register for classes. Many courses were already full, but Dr. Donmoyer recommended "Consulting to Groups," taught by Sister Theresa "Terri" Monroe, RSCJ. The course included the opportunity to serve as a teaching assistant (TA). Prior to my incarceration I had taken the same course, and Sister Terri graciously approved me to enroll as a TA for the doctoral section. There were about eight-five students enrolled, including eleven doctoral students who would be assigned to me.

As the Fall 2015 semester began, I was still on home confinement and struggling with self-doubt and shame. Sister Terri's trust in me was a gift. Her confidence began to restore my own. Looking back, I see that my temporary expulsion—painful though it was—was God's way of steering me toward this class and this remarkable woman. Sister Terri would become one of my most important mentors and friends. For more than a decade, she has offered me spiritual guidance, wisdom, and encouragement. What began as a course assignment became a life-altering relationship.

Once again, God provided a silver lining—transforming what felt like another setback into a source of grace and growth.

Probation

The federal correctional system abolished parole following incarceration in 1987, leaving probation as the only form of community supervision for federal offenders. Most state systems, unlike the federal, use both parole and probation. In some cases, for less serious offenses, probation is used as an alternative to incarceration, allowing the individual to remain in the community under supervision. Parole, on the other hand, always follows a prison sentence; a parolee is still considered in custody and for almost any violation can be returned to prison without a court hearing. A state probationer, unlike a parolee, remains under the jurisdiction of the courts and cannot be put into custody without a court hearing and ruling by a judge. In the federal system, probation functions as a hybrid—sometimes imposed instead of prison time, most often imposed following incarceration.

In my case, I was sentenced to three years of probation after my prison term. During my first semester back in graduate school, I was released from home confinement and officially began probation under the U.S. Probation Office for the Southern District of California. I reported to my assigned probation officer (PO) on October 14, 2015—twenty-four hours after my release from home confinement. My PO was a young man in his thirties, full of swagger and authority. He handed me paperwork, collected a urine sample, and reviewed the rules of supervision. He showed me a lot of "attitude," a schtick that I suspect he enacted with all new probationers. I had a bad feeling about him from the start, and my instincts proved correct.

Because my offense was nonviolent and I had stable housing, employment, and family support, I was classified as a low-risk probationer. I was not required to report regularly. Still, one week later, my PO called to tell me that my initial drug test was positive for methamphetamines. I was stunned. He ordered me to report immediately for another test. Panicked, I assumed the worst—that he would recommend that I return to prison. My panic may have been irrational, but I feared that this young officer was going to make life difficult for me.

Colette and I went to a private lab and paid $200 out of pocket for a hair test, which can detect drugs for up to a month. Three days later, the results came back: completely negative. When I showed the PO the report, he didn't apologize or even seem interested. Looking back, I believe he was simply testing my reactions—or toying with me.

A few weeks later, he showed up at my workplace. Flashing his badge in front of customers, he loudly asked for "Robert Ehnow" announcing that he was a probation officer. Mortified, I led him outside and told him that his public announcement was inappropriate and unprofessional. He just shrugged and said, "I don't care."

A few months later, that PO and another arrived for a scheduled home visit thirty minutes early. He was banging on the door while I was in the shower, followed by blowing up my cell phone with repeated calls. When I finally answered the door, dripping wet, he reprimanded me for not responding faster. These petty encounters became routine and exhausting. His attitude and behavior reflected an unfortunate truth: many in positions of authority within probation and parole view control as more important than support and compassion.

Fortunately, after six months, my case was transferred to "administrative status." My new PO, a kind and professional woman, immediately eased the tension. She told me I didn't need to report to her unless I had police contact and could travel anywhere in the United States without prior approval. For the next two and a half years, I remained on probation but spoke to her only once.

Ideally, probation or parole should provide both support and supervision—a bridge between incarceration and full reintegration. In practice, however, they often emphasize not guidance and rehabilitation, but control and intimidation. My early experience mirrored what many other returning citizens face: unnecessary obstacles that discourage rather than empower. For individuals without family support, education, or stable housing, such treatment can derail reintegration entirely. My faith tells me that society has a moral duty to help those concluding their incarceration to rebuild their lives with dignity. Employment, housing, and accountability are essential, but so are mercy and respect. When probationers or parolees fail, society itself fails. The cycle of incarceration continues, costs of reincarceration rises, and communities and families remain fractured.

My own reintegration was far from perfect, but I was blessed with unwavering support from family, friends, and my Church. In contrast, the state systems I have encountered—the Bureau of Prisons, the for-profit halfway house, and the probation office—did little to help and often made things harder. Yet God was present through it all, working quietly through the people who believed in me.

The next chapter continues this journey, exploring the essential elements of reintegration: healing, restoration, and forgiveness. God always provides what is needed, especially for those who open themselves to his grace. I didn't realize it then, but my reintegration was shaping me to embrace Christ's mission of love, mercy, and justice—for myself and for others seeking a successful path from prison to home.

Chapter 7

Hope Never Dies

Providing Hope

In 1981, Mehmet Ali Ağca attempted to assassinate Pope John Paul II. Though struck by two bullets, the pope survived and continued for nearly twenty-five more years until his death in 2005. From his hospital bed, John Paul II asked Catholics worldwide to pray for his assailant. Two years later, he met Ağca in prison and forgave him. In 2000, the pope requested that the president of Italy pardon Ağca, who was then released and extradited to Turkey. In 2007, Ağca converted from Islam and remains a Catholic today. Through forgiveness and mercy, John Paul II offered his would-be assassin a path to healing and salvation, embodying Christ's command to love our enemies and forgive those who harm us.

Pope Francis also displayed deep compassion for the incarcerated. During his first visit to the United States in 2015, one of his earliest stops was a prison near Philadelphia. Throughout his pontificate, he visited prisons in Italy, Mexico, Bolivia, Chile, and elsewhere—standing in solidarity with those society often forgets. Like John Paul II, Pope Francis modeled the gospel message of Matthew 25 and the corporal works of mercy, demonstrating that every human being possesses inherent dignity by virtue of being created in God's image.

In 2025 the Catholic Church marked a special year-long celebration, which Pope Francis designated as the "Jubilee Year of Hope." Such celebrations are scheduled every twenty-five years, though the pope may proclaim special jubilees, as Francis did in 2016 with the "Year of Mercy." The pope emphasized the Church's enduring commitment to the virtues of mercy, hope, forgiveness, and inclusion. Pope Leo XIV continues to emphasize these same values as he begins to lead the Church. The ideals of mercy and hope have been in short supply for prisoners, and as Christ's body the Church is in a position to reinforce these standards for the incarcerated.

During a Jubilee, the Holy Door at St. Peter's Basilica, a symbol of grace and renewal, is opened for pilgrims. During the Jubilee of Hope Pope Francis designated only one other official Holy Door at the Rebibbia New Complex Prison in Rome. Through this powerful gesture, the Church declared to prisoners that hope was not lost; it continues to inspire and to open up the pathway to rehabilitation.

Prisoners are often invisible to society, yet to God they remain fully seen and loved. Catholic Social Teaching emphasizes that every human life is sacred and imbued with dignity. Among God's people, one life does not rank above another. God loves equally the inmate on death row and the billionaire philanthropist. Human understanding finds God's equal love for the sinful and the pious paradoxical. Scripture and tradition, however, reveal that each person has value and dignity by virtue of being created in the image and likeness of God, and not from their profession or accomplishments.

Catholic Social Teaching centers upon the preferential option for the poor. In his ministry, Jesus focused on healing and uplifting those on the margins—the poor. Likewise, those who follow Jesus, the People of God, are called to live in communion with one another, providing for the material and spiritual needs of the poor and marginalized. Prisoners—often among society's poorest—are included in this call. Christians are summoned to go to the margins to minister, accompany, and love those in prison.

Accompanying prisoners paves a way to restoration and healing—for the prisoners and for their families—so they may feel welcomed, loved, and reintegrated into their communities. By forgiving his attacker, Pope John Paul II transformed a relationship born of violence into one of reconciliation; forgiving Mehmet Ali Agca allowed him to return to his community and ultimately to come to Christ. Pope Francis continued this legacy of forgiveness, proclaiming that every person, regardless of circumstance, deserves respect and mercy. Even those deemed unlovable or unforgivable remain beloved children of God, and the Church's mission is to extend healing and forgiveness to all.

Hope for the Condemned

In my office at the Diocese of San Diego, I keep a small framed portrait of John Wayne Thomson. He had been sentenced to death for multiple crimes, including murdering at least two people. Although Thomson received a death sentence, he did not die by an executioner's hand. After eighteen years on death row at San Quentin State Prison, he died of natural causes. Because he inflicted senseless violence on his victims, John Wayne Thomson deserved to spend the rest of his life in prison. Yet he also remained deserving of dignity as a human being. This truth reveals a profound tension in our faith: someone who denies others' dignity through violence and murder still retains dignity himself. This paradox rests in the mystery of God's "long game"—his patience and enduring hope that all humanity will return to him.

While on death row, Thomson returned to his Christian faith and, by all accounts, as a condemned prisoner, lived a quiet, devout life. He asked to be buried in a Catholic cemetery rather than at San Quentin, and my office fulfilled his request. He was laid to rest in a Catholic cemetery in San Diego. I hope John now lives eternally in one of the rooms God has prepared for each of his creatures. Though society had written him off as worthless, God never stopped calling or loving him. John's story illustrates why the Catholic Church revised its teaching on the death penalty. Previously, the Catechism of the Catholic Church stated that the death penalty could be used, but only in rare cases. After 2018 the Catechism was revised to state that it is never permissible. By executing a human being, the state claims authority over life and death, an authority incompatible with Catholic teaching that every human life is sacred and God is the sole source for all human life.

John Wayne Thomson spent the last two decades of his life in a maximum-security prison, with no possibility of parole and no opportunity to harm others in the outside world. His sentence was both just and restorative. It allowed him to reconcile with God and the Church—an opportunity he may have lost had his execution been carried out. Many faithful Christians still consider the death penalty to be a just punishment for heinous crimes. I, too, have wrestled with my position on this issue over the years, but I have come to believe that power over life belongs to God alone—not to the state or the executioner.

Thomson's framed portrait reminds me daily that every person has value and deserves dignity. It is never easy to forgive or love those who have inflicted great harm, yet that is exactly what Jesus asks of his followers. The People of God cannot limit hope to certain individuals or groups. Hope, one of the theological virtues, lives in each person, including the most vulnerable—even the condemned who seem undeserving. Christians do not pray only for those considered "good," but extend prayers to all, including those who have caused deep pain and suffering.

Journeying Toward Restoration

I had my first experience with restorative justice in 2001, when I was the executive officer—second in command—of a Marine Corps aviation logistics unit at Camp Pendleton. It was my first command-level position in a battalion- or squadron-sized unit. My commanding officer, Paul Callan, was renowned for his professionalism, intelligence, fairness, and physical fitness. I was honored that Paul asked me to serve as his executive officer while he commanded more than eight hundred Marines and Sailors. During our two years together, Paul spent significant time mentoring me and developing my own leadership capacity. He also introduced me—unknowingly at the time—to the principles of restorative justice.

In the military, a commanding officer has legal jurisdiction over service members for certain infractions, typically minor offenses such as unauthorized absences or disrespect toward a superior. The commanding officer can preside over an Article 15 hearing, commonly referred to as "non-judicial punishment" or "office hours." More serious offenses are referred to a court-martial, similar to a civilian criminal trial.

Our unit within the Marine Aircraft Group, included eight hundred men and women, with roughly six hundred of them under the age of twenty-five. Like their civilian counterparts, young Marines sometimes make poor decisions and find themselves in trouble. As the executive officer, I was responsible for maintaining good order and discipline for the commanding officer, so I was usually the first officer notified when a Marine violated an order or regulation. Paul, as commanding officer, decided how and when each case would be adjudicated. Most infractions were minor and handled through Article 15 hearings, where the Marine always had a choice—face the commanding officer or a panel of officers at a court-martial. Almost all chose to appear before the commanding officer.

Paul maintained high expectations and standards for every Marine under his command, and he balanced discipline with compassion. He was firm yet fair, holding each Marine accountable while upholding the morale and cohesion of the unit. What set Paul apart was his extraordinary commitment to restoration. After each hearing, he instructed the Marine's direct supervisors to support the individual's return to good standing within the unit. A few weeks later, Paul would personally visit the Marine's work center to check on his progress. These informal visits were compassionate and candid—acknowledging the Marine's mistake while reaffirming his worth. I was deeply impressed the first time I witnessed this. There are no manuals on how to treat a Marine after discipline has been administered, but if I were to write one, it would include Paul's consistent follow-up and personal care. His goal was to fully restore the Marine to the unit, sending a clear message that he still mattered.

Paul often went a step further by scheduling a run or walk with the Marine. This simple act epitomized companionship and acceptance. Running side by side, Paul demonstrated that rehabilitation and redemption were not theoretical, but real. His personal investment signaled that both he and the command had forgiven the Marine and welcomed him back. In essence, Paul's actions embodied restorative justice: accountability paired with compassion and reintegration.

Years later, when I became the commanding officer of a similar-sized unit, I borrowed Paul's "playbook." During one of my first Article 15 hearings in Iraq, our unit chaplain told me afterward that I had dispensed justice "in a biblical way." I took that as the highest compliment. Paul had modeled what justice and restoration should look like for young Marines—and for anyone who has gone astray.

It's no small detail that I asked Paul to hold me accountable while writing this book. He reviewed each chapter draft to ensure I met deadlines. It is also no coincidence that I asked Paul to write the foreword for this book as he accompanied me on my life journey through my divorce, my trial, my incarceration, and the writing of this book. Paul is a lifelong friend, a man of integrity, and someone I never want to disappoint. During my own trial, Paul served as a character witness; he never judged me, only supported me as a true Marine brother. Looking back, I see clearly that Paul's blend of accountability, compassion, and reintegration modeled a restorative approach to justice, even though at that time neither of us were even aware of the term restorative justice. My Marine Corps experience with Paul provided me with the clearest, most practical example of what restorative justice looks like in action.

The Restorative Police Officer and the Formerly Incarcerated Professor

Jeff Pace has been my friend for more than twenty-five years. For two years, we were neighbors in Chula Vista, California. Jeff has served as a police officer for over forty years—thirty with the San Diego Police Department and the last ten with the Chula Vista Police Department. Before that, he was a Marine Corps sergeant. Jeff is also one of my dearest family friends and an informal spiritual advisor. He can quote Scripture to fit any situation and exemplifies a life of faith, purpose, and virtue.

After my trial and conviction, Jeff was devastated when the news appeared in the local paper. Without hesitation, he reached out to Colette, offering his support. During my incarceration, Jeff regularly checked in with Colette and the kids and wrote me letters of encouragement. About six months before my release, he visited me at the prison in Colorado.

Jeff sometimes has a tough exterior persona. My father would have described him as "the kind of guy you wouldn't want to meet in a dark alley if you were up to no good," yet he possesses a compassionate heart filled with love for the Lord. He has worked in nearly every area of law enforcement—homicide, gang intervention, internal affairs, and patrol. For Jeff, policing is an extension of his commitment to serve God and God's people. His visit meant the world to me, especially knowing that he dislikes traveling unarmed to unfamiliar places. Jeff's visit was a complete act of love, and I was overjoyed to be the recipient of his love.

During that 2015 visit, Jeff introduced me to the concept of "restorative justice." He encouraged me to see my prison experience as something God could use to help others. He explained how restorative justice connects to community policing—collaborating with communities to build trust and safety and to support healing. Jeff mentioned that he worked with Dr. Alan Mobley, a San Diego State University criminology professor, who had also been formerly incarcerated. Jeff offered to connect us when I returned home, believing Alan would be a good mentor for my transition. That conversation planted a seed in me—a seed that, through—God's grace, would grow into a decade-long journey toward becoming a restorative justice practitioner and advocate.

Shortly after my release, while I was still on home confinement, Jeff made good on his promise and introduced me to Alan. He shared his remarkable story: once one of California's top cocaine traffickers in the 1980s, he had lived lavishly—beach house, Ferrari, and millions of dollars a year in profits from his criminal enterprise. Eventually, he was caught and sentenced to forty-five years in federal prison, at the time one of the longest sentences for a nonviolent drug offender. Fortunately for him, he was convicted before 1987. If he had been caught after 1987 when federal parole was abolished, then he would most probably still be in prison serving a forty-five-year sentence. He served ten years, during which he earned both bachelor's and master's degrees. After his release, he pursued a PhD in criminology at the University of California, Irvine, later becoming a criminology professor at San Diego State University.

Alan's story of redemption, resilience, and finding a pathway in higher education inspired me. He wanted to make the criminal justice system more humane and rehabilitative. I asked him to mentor me as I resumed my doctoral studies, and he readily agreed. We have been close friends ever since. Alan's journey is a remarkable story of rehabilitation and service through higher education during and after incarceration. He later invited me to help with a new program at San Diego State, "Project Rebound," which supports formerly incarcerated students. The program was founded in 1967 at San Francisco State University, by Dr. John Irwin, another formerly incarcerated criminologist. In 2015, the California Legislature expanded Project Rebound to other state universities, including San Diego State, where Alan became its first executive director.

At first, I agreed only to "check out" the Project Rebound program. But attending one of their meetings in spring 2016 moved me deeply. The students' resilience and commitment to rebuilding their lives were extraordinary. We met weekly in a circle to share our stories—of family, hardship, incarceration, and recovery. I spent two years with the group, volunteering regularly. Looking back, I see how clearly God's plan was unfolding. Through Jeff, Alan, and others, I was being prepared to serve. Project Rebound did not just give me an opportunity to help others—it was a profound awakening. The students were just like me: formerly incarcerated and seeking a new beginning through education. The courage of many who had faced harsher sentences and greater obstacles than I had inspired me. By 2018, several of these "Rebounders" graduated just as I completed my doctorate.

When I first left prison, I wanted nothing to do with the criminal justice system. I planned to move as far away from that world as possible. Yet through my friendship with Alan and my work at Project Rebound, I came to see that God was calling me to stand in solidarity with others who had been incarcerated. Alan's colleague, Dr. Dan Stacy—also formerly incarcerated and now a professor at San Diego State—guided and mentored me in this new, aspirational ministry. Through their mentorship and friendship, I learned about restorative justice from those who lived it. My initial post-incarceration plan, which did not involve doing any work around the criminal justice system, was beginning to unravel. God was moving me in a new direction, to serve those who have been or are currently incarcerated.

While volunteering at Project Rebound and completing my studies at the University of San Diego, I shifted my research focus. Initially, I planned to study issues facing military veterans, but Alan encouraged me to explore restorative justice instead. I ultimately centered my dissertation on prisoner reintegration and the role of higher education in reducing recidivism. Research shows that individuals who earn college or vocational degrees after incarceration have a recidivism rate of just 5 percent, compared to the national average of 60 percent. Education reduces the likelihood of reoffending by 55 percent.

This chapter and this book are not intended to be an academic deep dive into restorative justice, but rather a reflection on how relationships and others' compassion led me toward a life of service as a restorative justice practitioner. Through the genuine care and support of people like Dan, Jeff, and Alan, I learned to live restoratively—to combine accountability with empathy and to see God's presence in every act of reconciliation, healing, and growth.

After my release, God began preparing me to serve others who have been impacted by incarceration. In hindsight, I was being equipped to be the best version of myself, and that version was oriented to serve others. Sometimes God needs a "burning bush" to deliver his message, but most often speaks his message through others. Paul, Jeff, Alan, Dan and others not mentioned in this chapter were all such messengers and supporters. The next chapters explore what it means to live a restorative life, both professionally and spiritually. But first, I will detail my spiritual journey immediately following my release and the pivotal events that equipped me to serve others and work within the Church.

Spiritual Equipping

Earlier chapters described my spiritual journey during incarceration. Prison, unexpectedly, became a period of profound growth—a time to deepen my faith and discern what truly mattered. My prison experience marked the beginning of a psychological and spiritual shift toward accepting God's plan for me and my family: a plan to love God and everyone I might encounter.

Many incarcerated men and women experience similar awakenings. In prison, the basic needs of food, shelter, clothing, and work are met. Time—often scarce in the outside world—is abundant. Inside prison, ample time is one of the few luxuries, but it is a luxury only when used wisely. That time creates space for reflection, prayer, and spiritual renewal. Yet upon release, worldly concerns quickly reclaim priority.

When I left prison, I had a job waiting for me, a family eager to welcome me home, and a faith community ready to receive me. Still, that first year was spiritually challenging. I struggled to find time for prayer and to maintain the deep sense of faith I had developed inside. Colette and I also faced several lawsuits stemming from personally guaranteed loans tied to our failed business. I didn't want to focus on money any more than I had to, but financial stress tested my faith and my new priorities. I naively assumed that freedom would bring only brighter days, but reality proved otherwise.

One of our parish friends, Marybeth Parr, had long encouraged Colette and me to attend a Cursillo—a three-day Catholic retreat designed to renew faith and strengthen lay leaders. I had always found excuses not to go. But in the spring of 2016, a few months after I began volunteering with Project Rebound, I had run out of excuses and finally agreed. Married couples do not attend the same retreat. The men go one weekend followed by the women the next. Marybeth, our Cursillo sponsor, drove me to the retreat center in the mountains near Julian, about an hour northeast of San Diego. The retreat began Thursday evening and ended Sunday afternoon—seventy-two hours that would change me forever.

The Cursillo retreats, a "short course in Christianity" for lay Catholics, began in Spain during the 1940s. Today, it's a worldwide movement that helps participants rediscover faith and service. In San Diego, where the diocese offers two retreats every spring and another two every fall, it remains a vibrant movement, equipping lay leaders to evangelize and catechize others in their parish communities and throughout the diocese. It was no coincidence that I made my Cursillo less than a year after being released from prison. In reflection, it was exactly what I needed at that time in my life—a significant event in my own spiritual reintegration.

Although reluctant to go attend with men I did not know, I soon realized this was exactly what I needed. On the second evening, I experienced a profound *metanoia*—a conversion of heart. I shared with the retreat leader, through tears, the shame I carried from my incarceration and the harm it caused my family. For the first time, I released the emotional burden I had held for five years. On the final evening, I was invited to tell my story to about 150 men. I spoke openly about my fall from grace—from civic and military leader to disgraced inmate. I recounted how, as a commanding officer of more than a thousand Marines in Iraq, I could walk into a theater and everyone would rise to attention, a humbling sign of respect not for the man, but for the position. I told them how that former "somebody" now felt like a nobody. It was the first time I publicly shared my story of how failure, bankruptcies, and despair made my life difficult for me and my family.

That evening, my metanoia was nearly complete. I realized that God had surrounded me with men of integrity, whose kindness and budding friendship reflected God's mercy. The retreat leader assured me that I was not alone. He told me that the thousand men in the San Diego Cursillo movement would stand with me just as a thousand Marines once did. We often lose our way when we believe we must suffer alone, fearing judgment or rejection. But in truth, we need others—family, friends, and sometimes strangers—to remind us that we still matter. My Cursillo weekend renewed my faith through the love and fraternity of others.

Sometimes we must "connect the dots" between seemingly unconnected life experiences to recognize how God is at work in our lives. When I was leading prayer services in prison, we had musicians that would always conclude our service with the song "De colores," which literally means "of colors." It was a joke among our prison prayer group that our musicians always closed with the same song. At my Cursillo weekend, we were taught the lyrics of "De colores," the official Cursillo anthem, sung whenever men and women in the movement gathered. "De colores" represents being in God's grace, and it was no coincidence that I was introduced to the song while in prison. It is another reminder that God is working in my life all the time, and I, like others, need to pay attention and "connect the dots" of God's work in my own life.

Two months following my Cursillo retreat, Colette and I made a pilgrimage to the Holy Land led by Sister Terri Monroe, RSCJ, who I introduced in the last chapter. Sister Terri, a professor at the University of San Diego, had developed a course, "The Art of the Pilgrimage." As part of my graduate studies, I was required to take at least one international course. The course and our twelve-day journey to Israel and the West Bank fulfilled my international study requirement. Sister Terri with another Sacred Heart sister, Lyn Osiek, RSCJ, led nine graduate students, Colette, and me through the sacred sites of Judaism and Christianity. I was grateful that even though she was not a graduate student, Colette was allowed to join the pilgrimage; I sold the idea to Sister Terri that having a medical doctor with us on our pilgrimage would be prudent, and she agreed. Our small group was an eclectic community of pilgrims, including Catholics, Protestants, a Jew, and an atheist.

We began in Galilee, where Jesus started his public ministry. For six nights we stayed at the Mount of Beatitudes Guesthouse, run by Franciscan sisters, a perfect location for day trips to the places where Jesus preached and called his apostles. On our final day in Galilee, I spent some time in the Church of the Beatitudes, a modest chapel overlooking the Sea of Galilee. This is the site, it is believed, where Jesus preached his sermon on the mount that includes guideposts for living as a Christian, the eight beatitudes. Standing before that tranquil view, as my life flashed before me, I began to weep. In that moment, I felt God's unmistakable presence.

God called me by name and asked me to follow him. I can still recall the tears as I surrendered my plans to his will. My old life of ambition and self-direction was gone. God's plan, not mine, would guide my future. He had spoken, and this time, I truly listened. My metanoia was complete; I had surrendered. God calls each of us, though we often resist or doubt. Some may question whether what I experienced was real. But I know that God called me that day, and that moment changed everything—for me, for Colette, and for our family.

A New Beginning

My prison experience laid the foundation for a new beginning. I left prison with several goals: to finish my doctoral degree, rebuild my family's financial future, and move as far away from the system as possible. Of those three goals, I achieved only one. Three years after my release I completed my doctorate. The research and writing that consumed much of my time, became the springboard to a new life of service to the most marginalized members of society: the incarcerated. Through grace and my willingness to follow God's plan, I learned to embrace the dignity of all people, especially those who have been imprisoned.

In the Marine Corps, I learned that to be a good leader, you must love the Marines you lead. Now, I could say the same about my ministry: I love the incarcerated and formerly incarcerated men and women I encounter. Every good endeavor in life must begin with love. My calling is to serve them and their families with compassion and hope.

In the spring of 2018, I defended my dissertation before a committee of four professors who remain dear friends. My faculty advisor and committee chair, Dr. Bob Donmoyer, strongly supported my return to academia and served as my primary editor. Dr. Fred Galloway regularly checked in to see how I was doing as I navigated life back at the university. These two nationally respected scholars gave generously of their time and guidance. Sister Terri Monroe, my spiritual director, and Dr. Alan Mobley, my mentor from San Diego State University, also served on my committee. Each played a crucial role in my reintegration into the community, and I am blessed by their support.

Three weeks after defending my dissertation, I completed the final edits and formatting. Once I had uploaded the finished document to ProQuest and USD Digital, I officially became a published author. Yet within minutes of that accomplishment, I asked myself, *What's next*? I answered my own question—I probably had to get a job! My goal of completing my doctoral degree was accomplished; now I was asking God to assist me with finding meaningful, purposeful work.

God answered immediately. Within an hour of publishing my dissertation, I received an email from Father Mike Murphy linking to a job posting for an Associate Director of Restorative Justice at the Diocese of San Diego. The position required experience in prison ministry and a graduate degree—qualifications I met precisely. Excited, I met with Father Mike to discuss it further. I submitted my application, resume, and cover letter to the diocesan HR department. Weeks passed with no response. I followed up several times but heard nothing. Frustrated, I let Father Mike know that I had received no correspondence or phone calls even acknowledging they received my application.

A week later, during a separate meeting with the HR Director, Father Mike learned my application had been screened out because of my criminal record. Coincidently, the same meeting between Father Mike and the diocesan HR Director included was one of the guys, Gary, that sat at my table at my Cursillo retreat two years prior. Gary also interjected that the diocese should interview me for the position. Without their providential intervention, I might never have been interviewed for the job.

Two weeks later, while helping Sister Terri move from San Diego to northern California, I received a call; I had been offered the position. As Associate Director, I would oversee education, advocacy, and training for all restorative justice programs across the diocese, including ministry to twenty-four jails, prisons, and detention centers in San Diego and Imperial Counties. It was my dream job—one that perfectly united my faith, education, and lived experience.

Within a year, I was promoted to Director for the Office for Life, Peace, and Justice, a role I continue to hold. My initial goal—to rebuild financial stability for my family—remains a work in progress, but this position provides purpose, meaning, and provision. My family is returning to financial solvency, and our new goal is to use any surplus for God's work and his people. My third goal—to distance myself from the prison system—was never achieved. Instead, God led me closer to it, both professionally and spiritually. My life's work now focuses on supporting those who are incarcerated and after release helping their families as they rebuild.

My wife often says, "God does not call the equipped; He equips the called." That truth defines my life. My prison experience and spiritual conversion marked the beginning of my transformation. Every part of my life since—education, relationships, ministry—has equipped me to serve God and others. I emerged from prison broken but filled with hope. My studies in restorative justice deepened my understanding of healing and reconciliation, but it was my metanoia that truly empowered me to make a difference.

At the beginning of this chapter, I reflected on the mercy and hope that Popes John Paul II and Francis extended to those in prison—including John Paul II's forgiveness of the man who tried to kill him. Both exemplify how the theological virtue of hope sustains us in faith and leads us to charity. Hope allows us to persevere and see God's promise beyond the moment. In the movie, *Shawshank Redemption*, Andy (played by Tim Robbins), and Red (played by Morgan Freeman), are inmates that have differing views of hope. Red tells Andy that hope has no place inside prison, in fact Red refers to hope as a "dangerous thing." Andy later escapes and starts a new life on a beach in Mexico. After Red is released on parole, he finds a letter from Andy:

> Dear Red,
>
> If you're reading this, you've gotten out, and if you've come this far, maybe you're willing to come a little further. You remember the name of the town, don't you? I could use a good man to help me get my project on wheels. I'll keep an eye out for you and the chessboard ready. Remember, Red, hope is a good thing, maybe the best of things, and no good thing ever dies. I will be hoping that this letter finds you, and finds you well. Your friend,
>
> Andy

Later, inspired by Andy's message of hope, Red joins his friend in Mexico, ending the movie on a positive note.

Hope is indeed the best of things. It sustains the soul, redeems the fallen, and reminds us that no one—not even the condemned prisoner—is beyond God's love. The next chapter tells the stories of the formerly incarcerated who build hope among those they serve by providing housing and other elements of reintegration and reentry.

Chapter 8

A Community of Hope

Living as Community

Everyone belongs to a community. For most, family is the first and primary community. The family, often called the "domestic church," forms the foundation of the Church. Every person also belongs to other communities—a parish or faith community, workplace, neighborhood, or town. Community offers interaction, support for one another, and resolution of disagreements. It gives each person a shared sense of belonging and, ideally, a shared responsibility for one another.

One principle of Catholic Social Teaching (CST), subsidiarity, states that decisions and actions should be made at the lowest, most appropriate level. Subsidiarity empowers individuals and smaller groups to not rely on higher authorities, but to address issues directly. In the Church, for instance, decisions such as education for children or care for an elderly parent, should be made within the family before seeking guidance from the parish or diocese. Practicing subsidiarity where understanding and impact are greatest fosters responsibility.

Closely related to subsidiarity is another core principle of CST, solidarity. While subsidiarity focuses on responsibility at the local level, solidarity calls all members of society to work together for the common good. Though these principles can appear to be in tension, in practice they complement each other, promoting one of the Church's fundamental goals: unity. When local communities act responsibly within the broader context of solidarity, each principle strengthens the other. Together, these core tenets of CST support the gospel message and uphold the dignity of every human life, with a special concern for the poor and marginalized. CST is most effective when an entire community understands and lives out its principles.

Many religious orders, indigenous peoples, and cultures around the world, especially in Africa and Asia, naturally understand the value of community. In contrast, Americans often lack a deep appreciation for community belonging, perhaps because of the declining value placed on the family as society's first community. Not long ago, dining alone was unusual; today, "table for one" is common. This diminished sense of community may also stem from an emphasis on individual liberty and the romanticized idea of rugged individualism that shaped the early history of the United States. Western films celebrating the lone hero still resonate deeply with many Americans. Whatever the cause, this weaker sense of community is a particularly American phenomenon.

Prison, however, is a unique kind of community. Each and every member—inmates, correctional officers, and staff—plays a role in maintaining safety and order. Prisons are self-contained communities, providing food, clothing, shelter, employment, and rehabilitative programming. Inmates cook, serve, clean, work, and even teach programs to help others prepare for reentry into society. In California, inmate leaders often facilitate violence prevention, advocate for better conditions, and help maintain order. Ironically, prisoners may understand the essence and value of community better than many Americans who have never lived in such a structured, interdependent environment.

Those who spend many years in prison often become "institutionalized," deeply dependent on the order and rhythm of that community. Upon release, they still need structure and community to reintegrate successfully into society. Research suggests that what happens in the first three to six months after release determines whether recently released prisoners succeed or fail with reentry. Former prisoners often fail because they leave a structured, supportive community inside prison walls and return to an outside community without structure or support.

Building the Idea of Community for Returning Citizens

When I began working for the Diocese of San Diego, I inherited a robust, beautiful prison ministry. My predecessor, Deacon Jim Walsh, had built a dedicated team of more than four hundred volunteers providing Catholic religious services in the twenty-five jails, prisons, and detention facilities across the diocese. He also partnered with several nonprofit organizations to support returning citizens as they reintegrated into society. As I assessed the diocesan prison ministry, I hoped to expand it by creating a reentry program that included transitional housing for men and women recently released from jail or prison. My motivation was personal. My own transitional housing experience had been subpar; it did little to address the immediate needs of those transitioning from prison to society.

I shared my idea with my immediate supervisor at the time, Auxiliary Bishop John Dolan. He was open to my proposal, and suggested I visit a building owned by St. John the Evangelist Parish in central San Diego. The U.S. Marshals Service had used the property, a former convent, to house women who had been victims and offenders of sex trafficking. When Robert McElroy became the diocesan bishop in 2015, he ended the arrangement with the Marshals Service, believing it improper that church property be used as a detention facility. Catholic Charities of San Diego later repurposed the building as a home for female victims of sexual trafficking and violence. That program lasted a few years but eventually closed due to financial challenges.

Early in 2019 I visited the former convent for the first time. The building had been vacant for several months and was in poor condition. Still, I felt hopeful that it could be transformed into a transitional house for returning citizens. The building could accommodate up to thirty-eight residents, was centrally located, and had access to public transportation. Although I had no formal plan or prior experience with housing projects—and the project was outside my primary duties at the diocese—I began visiting transitional houses throughout San Diego to learn what a successful program needed. I also sought a service provider willing to partner with the diocese to manage the envisioned facility.

One evening later that year, I attended an event at the American Civil Liberties Union (ACLU) San Diego Chapter for formerly incarcerated individuals. I had been attending these ACLU meetings for several months, connecting with men and women actively supporting those recently released from prison. These informative and deeply enriching meetings offered me opportunities to learn from others impacted by the criminal justice system. During one meeting, attendees were invited to share updates on their projects. I mentioned that my office was exploring a transitional housing initiative for recently released inmates.

Some moments clearly reveal the hand of God at work. That evening at the ACLU was one of them. I boldly announced to a group of about ten people that my office planned to open a transitional house for returning citizens at St. John the Evangelist Parish in the Hillcrest area of San Diego. At the time, I had no agreement with the parish, no permission from the bishop, and no experience running a housing initiative. When I finished speaking, the man next to me asked pointedly, "What do you know about transitional housing, dawg?" I replied, "I don't know anything about transitional housing—but I'm going to open one at St. John the Evangelist in Hillcrest!"

That evening, the idea of building a transitional house—and, more importantly, a community of hope—was born. The man who had challenged me was George Chappell, a formerly incarcerated gang member who had managed transitional housing for a local nonprofit. When we met, he had recently opened his own transitional house for men in National City, between San Diego and Chula Vista. George invited me to tour his facility, and I accepted. That visit marked the beginning of a lasting partnership and friendship. Together, we began building a small but vital piece of God's Kingdom—a community of hope for those who had nearly lost hope.

Closing the Margins

Some individuals and communities live outside the mainstream on the margins, lacking the essentials of steady employment, safe housing, healthcare, and opportunities for growth. The homeless, the working poor, the formerly incarcerated, and many newly arrived immigrants live in this reality.

In Matthew 25, Jesus identifies these people—the homeless, prisoners, the hungry and thirsty, the stranger, and the sick—as the focus of his ministry. The People of God are called to close the gap between the margins and the mainstream by standing in solidarity with the marginalized.

They do this through small acts of charity and larger efforts that address the root causes of poverty and exclusion. Before their incarceration most prisoners lived on the margins, and upon their release will return there.

At the margins, Christ presents himself in these less fortunate brothers and sisters. Going to the margins, fulfills Jesus' command: "Truly, I tell you, just as you did it to one of the least of these brothers and sisters of mine, you did it to me" (Mt 25:40). Such encounters transform everyone involved—those living in comfort and those living in need. True charity transcends meeting physical needs; it changes hearts, both giver and receiver. Through these sacred encounters, both experience the true gift of charity—a conversion of hearts.

To understand the lived experiences of those who reside at the margins it is necessary to go there. Genuine encounter generates an understanding that starts to close the gap between the marginalized and the rest of society. Once their struggles are appreciated, meaningful action can be taken to bring them closer into the mainstream. I know personally what it means to live on the margins. Prisoners and their families occupy a distinct place outside the mainstream—physically and psychologically. Those on the margins often carry seemingly unbearable loads, including homelessness, addiction, hunger, and mental illness.

The incarcerated and formerly incarcerated often bear an invisible but real scarlet letter—an "F" for felon. Society permanently closes many doors to those who carry this mark. With few opportunities and limited social capital, they often remain isolated at the edges. I know that most men and women returning from prison want to live stable, normal lives, but society places obstacles in their way. Successful reintegration requires safe housing and steady employment, but those with a felony conviction cannot easily obtain either. My ministry's mission has been—and remains—to close the gap between the formerly incarcerated and the rest of society.

Over the next eighteen months, the vision of providing safe, comfortable transitional housing for men recently released from prison was nourished, refined, and made real. George Chappell and I partnered to bridge the divide between the mainstream and the marginalized—one parish community at a time in San Diego.

The Kairos House of San Diego

Humans live within linear, measurable time—what the Greeks called "chronos." Yet there is another kind of time, measured not by minutes but by divine moments and opportunities: "Kairos," or God's time.

I initially thought of calling our transitional housing project "The Matthew 25 House." But when Bishop Dolan suggested "Kairos House," I immediately liked the name. It echoed the well-known Kairos Prison Ministry, a national program in more than three hundred prisons across the United States that adapts the Catholic Cursillo retreat model to evangelize inmates. This non-denominational retreat transforms thousands of lives each year. It indeed was "kairos time"—God's time—that guided our idea and brought the project to life.

While George and I were pursuing the project in chronos time, George's friend and business partner, Eddie Blajos, had already been living for many years in kairos time. I met Eddie in the spring of 2019, shortly after I met George at the ACLU session. George and Eddie had founded Restoring Citizens, the organization behind their first transitional house in National City. If the term "OG" (Original Gangster) ever truly fit someone, it would be Eddie. A former leader in the Mexican Mafia, his early life story was filled with violence, revenge, and prison political power. Eddie was born into Los Angeles gang culture, and his family had a long history with the Mexican Mafia. His cousin Art Blajos, wrote *Blood In, Blood Out*, which depicts Art's story in the Mexican Mafia and later his reconciliation as a man of faith. Art Blajos' story parallels the life story of his cousin and my friend, Eddie Blajos.

At age seventeen, Eddie was sentenced to life without the possibility of parole. In prison he became a leader within the Mexican Mafia. For twenty-eight years, he lived in that world as expected—violent, feared and unrepentant. Then one day, at a prison program, a woman shared her story as a survivor of violence. Her testimony pierced Eddie's heart. Soon after, he renounced gang life and chose to follow God.

Renouncing gang life comes at a terrible cost. His former associates warned him, and when he did leave the Mexican Mafia they stabbed him twenty-eight times, leaving him for dead in his cell. For eight hours Eddie lay in a pool of blood before correctional officers took him away for medical care. During his recovery, he made a vow to serve God and others for the rest of his life. Over the next fourteen years, he became a model inmate and peacemaker, deeply respected even by those who once opposed him.

In 2013, California changed its sentencing laws, making juvenile life without parole sentences retroactively eligible for review. After forty-two consecutive years in prison, Eddie was paroled in 2017. Two years later, eighteen months after his release, I met him. He became not only a friend but also one of my most trusted spiritual mentors. Despite his troubled past, Eddie radiated peace and spiritual strength. I knew we were meant to be friends and partners in this mission.

Eddie, a man of character, full of compassion, spiritual strength, and unconditional love, spent most of his life behind bars. In addition to the forty-two straight years in prison, he spent almost a decade in and out of juvenile detention facilities. I have modeled my work on his resilience and faith. His life provided me the spiritual inspiration to make Kairos House a reality that would serve men coming home from prison.

George brought business insight and entrepreneurial drive; Eddie brought spiritual depth and unwavering faith. I felt blessed to be along for the ride. Together, we committed to creating a home for men returning from incarceration—a community of hope. George, Eddie, and I shared the same painful common experience: transitional housing that was disorganized, exploitative, and devoid of dignity. Our time in prison had taught us the value of structure and respect, qualities sorely missing from most reentry programs. We were determined to build something better.

The creation story of the Kairos House testifies to how the Holy Spirit moves unexpected people to fulfill God's work. Eddie, George, and I responded to God's call to serve those most in need—men seeking housing and a second chance. When I and the diocesan director for Catholic Charities, Vino Pajanor, visited Restoring Citizens' house in National City, we were struck by how well-run it was compared to others we had toured. It stood out as a model. Vino suggested that we partner with Restoring Citizens for our own transitional home.

That partnership soon took shape. Restoring Citizens and the Office for Life, Peace, and Justice at the Diocese of San Diego joined to create a model transitional house. St. John the Evangelist Parish, the building's owner, would serve as the landlord. My office acted as liaison between the parish, the diocesan Real Estate Services Corporation, and Restoring Citizens. The parish administrator, Father Kevin Casey, SJ, was cautious but optimistic. Although other organizations, including Jewish Family Services, had expressed interest in the property, Father Casey believed our vision best aligned with the parish's mission. Father Casey was patient with us because he personally wished that we would succeed in helping men who were clearly on the margins.

Renovating the building required more than $200,000, an enormous sum for a small parish with limited resources. Still, the parish remained committed. I explored outside funding options, but it became clear that one group's interest was not altruistic, but profit-driven. We declined their offer, choosing to rely solely on parish and diocesan support. By 2020, the COVID-19 pandemic added uncertainty to an already fragile project. George and I began to wonder if the Kairos House would ever become a reality. The renovation took more than a year, and some questioned whether Restoring Citizens had the capacity to expand its program by 300 percent. Eddie, however, never doubted. His faith in God's timing sustained us.

In 2020, as George and I struggled with uncertainty, Eddie reassured us that the Kairos House would come to fruition. He believed God's will was already at work, and he was right. The Kairos House gave George, Eddie, and me the opportunity to work together in San Diego to bring returning citizens back from the margins.

By December 2020, Restoring Citizens' contract with San Diego County Probation was renewed and expanded, providing the funding needed to make the Kairos House sustainable. As far as I know, George and Eddie are the only formerly incarcerated gang members to have a housing contract with a county probation office in the state of California. In early 2021, Restoring Citizens signed a lease with St. John the Evangelist Parish. By April, the first residents arrived. George and I had doubted, but Eddie's unwavering faith carried the project forward. The Kairos

House of San Diego—born of faith, perseverance, and God's perfect timing—finally opened.

Creating a Home

When George, Eddie, and I left prison, each of us was assigned to a transitional house in San Diego County. Our experiences were uniformly poor. Most transitional houses focused on control, supervision, and collecting residents' paychecks rather than helping them rebuild their lives. Our partnership between Restoring Citizens and the Office for Life, Peace, and Justice aimed to change that. Together, we created not just a house but a *home*—a place where men recently released from prison could find belonging, stability, and dignity.

A true home meets physical, emotional, and spiritual needs. It offers not only shelter but also companionship, mutual support, and brotherly love. The Kairos House of San Diego was intentionally designed to foster that environment. Although the building was zoned for up to thirty-eight residents, we limited occupancy to thirty-one. We refused to warehouse people. Each room houses two residents, except for two larger rooms that can accommodate four. The Kairos House was created to provide the tender needs of companionship, brotherly love, and spiritual nourishment. We created a community of men within the community of faith in the parish.

The Kairos House also has its own chapel, with stained-glass windows, an altar, an ambo, and seating for twenty-one worshippers. The chapel, once converted into a bedroom during previous uses of the building, was restored to a sacred space for prayer and worship. George and Eddie allowed me to lead the effort to refurbish it, and my diocesan office provided modest funds for the restoration.

I have been blessed to pray in sacred spaces around the world—from the basilicas of Rome to the Church of the Holy Sepulchre in Jerusalem. Yet the simple chapel inside the Kairos House remains my favorite. It is sacred ground because its mission—to heal and restore—is holy work, blessed by God.

The Kairos House also includes a spiritual care team. My friend, Father Mike Ravenkamp, SJ, was involved from the beginning, serving as chaplain and through his presence setting the spiritual tone. Legally blind, Father Mike possesses a unique insight—he sees the goodness in everyone, even those who have caused great harm. In the first two years of operation, Father Mike established the spiritual care team; his example of ministry, listening, talking, and simply being present for the residents, continues to this day.

Over the past five years, several deacon candidates have joined the spiritual care team as part of their pastoral formation, serving those who are poor and formerly incarcerated. The team also includes an Ignatian Volunteer Corps member and, more recently, Father Paul Griesgraber, a retired priest from the Archdiocese of Los Angeles, who faithfully attends the Sunday evening AA/NA community meetings.

The Kairos House is exceptionally clean, well-managed by Restoring Citizens, and respected by both county probation and the San Diego Police Department. George and Eddie maintain collaborative relationships with law enforcement, earning trust through transparency and accountability. The success of the Kairos House, I believe, lies in its spiritual foundation. George and Eddie know that they were given a second chance, and their faith permeates the program, shaping it into a place of redemption, discipline, and grace. The residents are greeted with brotherly love for men who need structure, community, and patronage.

The Kairos House has also hosted multi-day immersion programs for diocesan seminarians. These visits allow them to meet residents, learn about their struggles, and celebrate Mass with them in the chapel. They also cook meals and share time with the men, breaking down barriers and fostering mutual respect. The Kairos House is a force-multiplier for faith, understanding, and compassion at both the parish and diocesan levels.

The house has welcomed volunteers from the University of San Diego, local chapters of the Knights of Columbus, and the Order of Malta, among others. Our auxiliary bishops have celebrated Mass there, and my office hosts special dinners for Thanksgiving, Christmas, and Easter. Through these acts of accompaniment, the Church shows our brothers at the Kairos House that they are not forgotten—they are members of our community, worthy of dignity and love. Our Catholic community in San Diego has embraced the mission of the Kairos House, working together to lift up our brothers and support their physical and spiritual needs.

A Model for Community

The staff and residents of the Kairos House deeply understand the value of community. All have experienced structured communal life within prison walls, and they bring that understanding into their new environment. The Kairos House is closely connected to the larger communities of St. John the Evangelist Parish and the Hillcrest neighborhood in San Diego through many acts of shared support.

Local parishioners and community members donate quality clothing that residents can wear to job interviews and in daily life. Volunteers from the diocesan Creation Care Team have planted gardens and fruit trees on the property. A friend from the Cursillo community, who owns a cabinet manufacturing company, built custom cabinets and a new dining table for the residents' common areas. One of our deacon candidates, who owns a roofing company, installed a new roof at cost. These acts of generosity exemplify the change of heart that occurs when a faith community truly embraces those who have lived on the margins.

Every Sunday, all residents, staff, and volunteers gather after dinner for a community meeting. Formally, it is an AA/NA meeting, but in spirit, it is much more—a time to strengthen the bonds of brotherhood and accountability. Father Paul Griesgraber and members of the spiritual care team often attend to listen, encourage, and discern the residents' needs, both material and spiritual.

George Chappell intentionally calls these gatherings "community meetings" rather than recovery meetings. The discussions address issues important to everyone in the house—residents, staff, and volunteers alike. These meetings reinforce shared responsibility and foster mutual understanding, helping residents take ownership of their community and growth.

The Kairos House began as an idea and, through prayer, perseverance, and the generous collaboration of parish and diocesan partners, became a living reality. The Church most powerfully proclaims the Gospel when it works to close the gap between the mainstream and the margins. The Kairos House embodies the foundation of Catholic Social Teaching: the dignity of every human person.

The principle of solidarity is visible in the partnership between the parish, the diocese, and the Hillcrest neighborhood. Subsidiarity is lived daily through the residents and staff, who make decisions that directly affect their community. The Kairos House stands as a vivid example of how Catholic Social Teaching—in action—promotes human dignity, mercy, forgiveness, and love. While no transitional house is perfect, the Kairos House of San Diego offers a model for what is possible when faith, compassion, and community converge. Some residents must leave due to relapse or rule violations, but even then, the door remains open for those who wish to return once they are ready.

The collaboration between Restoring Citizens, St. John the Evangelist Parish, and the Diocese of San Diego demonstrates how the Church can partner with local organizations to live out its mission—bridging the divide between the mainstream and the marginalized. The Kairos House of San Diego is indeed holy ground, a sacred space where God's mercy, human dignity, and community come together in living witness to the Gospel.

The following chapter introduces a restorative practice known as "Council" or "circles," a methodology for constructive, meaningful dialogue. Increasing polarization and lack of respect have challenged the Church and other institutions, and they are grappling with inherent distrust among the people they are supposed to serve. Council or circle has been successfully used in a myriad of settings in my ministry where I serve in the diocese.

Chapter 9

Circle Up

Not Listening

Part of my post-incarceration experience has been with a restorative practice known as "circles" or "Council." Circles are facilitated gatherings that promote community-building, conflict resolution, and collaborative problem-solving. Council is a specific circle practice that I studied, and I later became an instructor in the method. In this chapter, I will use the terms Council and circles interchangeably. The positive, meaningful communication that they foster provides opportunities to reduce polarization and misunderstanding among individuals and groups.

My involvement began shortly after my release from prison, while volunteering with formerly incarcerated university students. Over the past ten years, my experience as both a participant and facilitator has expanded to include work with incarcerated men, formerly incarcerated men and women, and Catholic faithful across the Diocese of San Diego. This work took on new meaning during the Synod on Synodality, initiated in 2021 under the guidance of Pope Francis. American culture does not emphasize the value of listening. This is not a criticism but an observation of a defining national trait. Americans are a people of action—driven by movement, innovation, and results. This spirit of determination and ingenuity helped the United States grow as a nation in the nineteenth century and emerge as a global superpower in the twentieth. Listening, discernment, and relationship-building are not America's strongest suits. Similarly, throughout much of its history, the Catholic Church has not been a listening Church. At times, often in response to external pressures, it has embraced dialogue, but only sporadically. For centuries, the Church's norm has been its hierarchical structure and top-down decision-making. At the diocesan level, Catholics expect bishops to lead and make most decisions. Likewise, at the parish level, the faithful often rely on the pastor to determine priorities in ministry, finances, and liturgy. Ironically, even though American Catholics are deeply shaped by democratic ideals they widely accept this less democratic form of governance.

For Christians, God is relational. The Trinity—Father, Son, and Holy Spirit—is a perfect communion of eternal love. God's deepest desire is that his creatures receive this love and return it to him and to one another. To grow and endure, relationships require patience, understanding, and charity, qualities that emerge through listening and dialogue. God comes to be known most intimately through prayer and the sacraments. Through prayer God's creatures listen and speak with him; likewise, they grow closer to one another by listening and communicating sincerely. Many human relationships suffer because they lack a foundation of mutual understanding born of true listening. Listening deeply with attentive presence affirms that the other person matters, and expresses love and respect.

American culture prizes results and action. Listening is often valued principally as a means to gather information for decision-making. Yet the deeper purpose of listening is to build strong, trusting relationships. Throughout my professional life—as a Marine Corps officer, business owner, and now a leader within a religious nonprofit organization—I have learned that authentic relationships lead to effective action and produce meaningful results. Without listening and dialogue, such relationships cannot function. Early in my career, I focused entirely on performance and outcomes; my listening skills were limited because I measured success by results.

We are living in a time of deep division, both politically and socially. When I started working for the Diocese of San Diego in 2018, I quickly realized that divisions within the Church mirrored those in society. American Catholics are often polarized into progressive and conservative camps, and both sides can resist genuine listening and dialogue. Soon after I began working at the diocese, two major crises in American Catholicism erupted: the release of the Pennsylvania Grand Jury report and the revelations about Cardinal Theodore McCarrick's years of abuse and sexual misconduct. The Pennsylvania Grand Jury Report released in 2018, documented decades of Catholic clergy sexual abuse of minors in six Pennsylvania dioceses. For years Cardinal McCarrick, Archbishop Emeritus of Washington, had credible allegations of sexual misconduct with seminarians and others, and Church officials took no significant action. These events reignited widespread anger and mistrust toward Church leadership.

The Diocese of San Diego had faced its own reckoning in 2007, when it filed for bankruptcy amid numerous historical claims of clerical sexual abuse. The diocese paid $198 million to settle 140 cases. At the time, it was the second largest such settlement in U.S. Church history. While no credible allegations have arisen in the Diocese of San Diego for more than two decades, the national scandals reopened old wounds and moral outrage.

In the fall of 2018, Bishop Robert McElroy undertook a diocesan listening tour, a courageous effort to hear the pain and frustration of the faithful. Unfortunately, the sessions bore only limited fruit. I attended two and found them chaotic, resembling more like the Jerry Springer show, than experiences of meaningful dialogue. Few participants seemed interested in truly listening either to one another or to the bishop. I began to wonder if the circle method I had been using with formerly incarcerated people could offer a more fruitful, respectful approach to constructive conversations on painful topics.

The Way of Council

About six months after my release from prison, I began volunteering with Project Rebound, a support program a for formerly incarcerated students at San Diego State University (SDSU). I had no idea what to expect. I assumed I would simply assist my friend Dr. Alan Mobley, the program's executive director, in getting the new initiative off the ground. On my first day, however, I found myself sitting in a circle with several undergraduate and graduate students, all formerly incarcerated. Each of us had the opportunity to speak and share what was happening in our lives. We used a "talking piece": the person holding it spoke while everyone else listened. When finished, the speaker passed it to the next person, who then in turn shared.

I had no prior experience with the communication practice known as Council or Circles, but I was deeply moved by that first gathering. Listening to the stories of these students—men and women who had endured incarceration and were now pursuing higher education—touched me deeply. I decided to continue volunteering, and I quickly realized that the experience was giving me far more than I could ever give back. Through this ancient practice of listening and storytelling, I formed genuine friendships and discovered spiritual and emotional healing. I realized that my own journey was not unique but part of a shared human story.

Dr. Alan Mobley and his colleague Dr. Dan Stacy, both professors at SDSU, had themselves been incarcerated. They modeled purpose and compassion for students on their own educational journeys. Over the next year, I regularly sat in Council, not as a leader or facilitator, but as an equal participant who shared both my vulnerabilities and my strengths. This period was rich in learning and love. I began to see my time in prison not as an experience to erase but as an invitation to transformation. Council gave me the space to listen with compassion, to dialogue honestly, and to recognize that I am connected with others through shared life experiences.

So what is Council, and what are circles? These methods are both ancient and contemporary, practiced across cultures and faith traditions and rooted in the natural world. They create an experience of true community, recognizing that each person's story carries part of a greater truth. They foster deep, relational communication through attentive, compassionate listening and honest, spontaneous speech. They allow space for insight, wisdom, and healing—both personal and collective. In essence, Council or circle are structured ways of listening and speaking that empowers all participants as equal contributors.

Both use a talking piece, often a meaningful personal or community item, that symbolizes the right to speak. Whoever holds it has the permission and authority to speak, while all others listen. It is passed around the circle to encourage each participant to share their story and their reflections on the chosen topic. Council operates through shared agreements rather than rigid rules. Participants commit to speaking from the heart, listening without judgment, expressing themselves concisely, and sharing spontaneously. Confidentiality is essential; what is shared in the circle stays in the circle. Topics are usually framed by questions that invite personal storytelling rather than abstract discussion, and heart-centered dialogue rather than head-centered debate.

Council became a lifeline for me. After prison, when I returned to the University of San Diego for graduate school, I carried significant trauma and shame, yet the university offered no space to address those wounds. Project Rebound's use of Council created a safe environment where students could talk about their experiences with the criminal justice system. I immediately recognized its value. Many of the students had been incarcerated for years, even decades, and through Council we built deep, enduring bonds and friendships that continue more than ten years later.

Council is not a "New Age" invention, as some might think. It is an ancient method for fostering honest, sometimes difficult communication within a safe and respectful container. The circular seating arrangement itself minimizes hierarchy and emphasizes equality. Although a facilitator usually guides the process, he or she is also a participant and witness. All participants share responsibility for the dialogue and agree to confidentiality before beginning. In my experience, the circle's structure reduces polarization, misunderstanding, and domination by any one person or group. When practiced with intention and mutual respect, it offers a profound alternative to conventional forms of communication that too often breed conflict.

Intrigued by the power of Council, I began formal training to become a facilitator. I studied at the Ojai Foundation in Ojai, California, a sanctuary for seekers and scholars dedicated to deep listening, purposeful dialogue, and spiritual growth. Although I was then a Ph.D. student among many accomplished scholars at the Ojai Foundation, I felt right at home. During weekend retreats on the Foundation's grounds, I learned that Council is more than a communication technique; it is a way of life. Grounded in spiritual traditions from many faiths, it resonated deeply and aligned seamlessly with my Catholic spirituality.

Eventually, I pursued the path of becoming a "carrier of Council"—someone who not only lives by its principles but also brings them to others. For two years, I apprenticed under my mentor, Yamin Chehin, who challenged me to embody Council in every part of my life. Her simple instruction —"carry Council in your bones"—remains with me. I was also mentored by Jack Zimmerman, co-author with Gigi Coyle of *The Way of Council*. In hindsight, I was richly blessed with Yamin's mentorship and Jack's guidance, as I journeyed on my path to be a carrier of Council. Their guidance was providential preparation for the work God later called me to do in the Church.

Today, I am both a carrier of Council and a certified facilitator and trainer with the International Institute of Restorative Practices (IIRP). This ten-year journey has transformed how I listen. I now do my best to approach every conversation with openness and the intention to listen without judgment, and without planning my next response. This practice has resulted in life feeling fuller for me, and communication deeper, more authentic, and less divisive. Council is practiced in prisons, schools, faith communities, and even corporate settings. For me, it is more than a communication method—it is a spiritual encounter that I continue to live daily in my professional, personal, and faith life.

Synod on Synodality

One day during the summer of 2021, Bishop McElroy walked into my office and asked me to serve on the diocesan commission for synodality. I immediately agreed. When I was a Marine, I learned that when the boss asks you to do something, as long as it is legal and moral, you say yes. Bishop McElroy explained that he wanted me to focus on three marginalized groups: the incarcerated and formerly incarcerated, the homeless, and immigrants and asylum seekers. After he left, I realized I didn't fully understand what "synodality" meant. I knew that bishops occasionally gather in meetings called "synods" and that under Bishop McElroy's leadership our diocese had held two, one on family life in 2016 and another on youth and young adults in 2019. As I began to read, I discovered that synodal gatherings have long been part of the Church's tradition, most recently in South America, where Pope Francis served as priest, bishop, and cardinal before becoming pope.

In the Catholic Church, bishops meet with the Holy Father at a synod to discuss matters of faith, doctrine, and governance. The word itself means "assembly" or "meeting." The early Church councils, such as those of Jerusalem and Nicaea, were synods. Since Vatican II, bishops have gathered about every three years for synods, and the pope may also convene special ones on particular themes—such as the Synod on the Amazon in 2019, in which Bishop McElroy participated. Through my research, I understood the purpose of synods generally, but I still wasn't sure what a synod on synodality meant and how it applies to gatherings of lay people as well as of bishops. I learned that synodality means listening and discerning together so that all baptized faithful can participate more fully in the Church's mission, and when appropriate, in its governance.

A week after the bishop had asked me to serve on the synod commission, I received a formal letter confirming my appointment—and naming me as co-chair alongside our diocesan chancellor, Marioly Galván. Bishop McElroy hadn't mentioned the co-chair role, but as he was the boss, I accepted the assignment and set out to learn everything I could about synodality. I immersed myself in Vatican documents and papal writings to gain a deeper understanding of the process. I was also grateful to work alongside Marioly, one of the most organized, capable, and joyful people I have ever known.

One of my primary responsibilities was to help design the process by which synod participants would listen and dialogue with one another. Naturally, I thought of Council and its circle method. I wasn't sure how the idea would be received, as some might see Council as a "new age," overly informal practice that does not align with Catholic practices. Nevertheless, I proposed using the circle model as the foundation for our diocesan synod sessions,and the method was accepted by Bishop McElroy and the commission. The global Synod on Synodality began in fall 2021, with dioceses expected to conduct their own listening sessions by spring 2022 and submit reports to their national bishops' conferences by June. It was an ambitious timeline. Pope Francis asked Catholics, and even some non-Catholics, to listen and dialogue on three themes: their joys, sorrows, and hopes in the life of the Church.

The Diocese of San Diego held its synod sessions in March and April 2022, using the circle method to guide conversation around these three themes. Small group circles took place across San Diego and Imperial Counties in parishes, prisons, homeless shelters, and other venues. More than eleven thousand people participated in over fourteen hundred circles. Designated scribes recorded insights—an unusual step for Council gatherings, but essential for data collection. To help analyze the results, the diocese engaged faculty from the University of San Diego and San Diego State University. Looking back, I'm still amazed that our diocese managed to coordinate such an extensive effort across more than one hundred parishes, prisons, homeless shelters, and other sites in only a few months. It was a Holy Spirit–guided accomplishment made possible by Bishop McElroy's vision and the dedication of countless diocesan and parish leaders.

The Diocese of San Diego soon gained national attention for its synodal efforts, a mixed blessing. The recognition affirmed that we were doing the work Pope Francis and Bishop McElroy had called for, yet it also brought new expectations and responsibilities. In 2023, we held another diocesan-wide synod, this time focused on the Eucharist, the source and summit of the Catholic faith. In many ways, this second synod was even more fruitful. It centered on three questions: Describe a meaningful experience you or someone close to you has had in participating in the Eucharist, describe a challenge you or someone close to you has faced related to the Eucharist, and as you leave this experience, how can you be the living presence of Jesus in your parish and community? This second diocesan-wide synod took place within the National Eucharistic Revival, which was an opportunity for the U.S. Catholic Church to renew a love and understanding of the Holy Eucharist.

While delegates from around the world were gathering in Rome for the global synod, we were hosting small group dialogues throughout San Diego and Imperial Counties. The Eucharistic Synod drew more than fourteen thousand participants over forty-five days in nearly two thousand small group circles; about six thousand of the participants were youth and young adults. The findings were rich and inspiring. I believe the Diocese of San Diego engaged more participants than any other diocese in the United States—and possibly the world. At the synod, the circle method proved an ideal way for Catholics to share their experiences and hopes for the Church. Bishop McElroy's vision, combined with the enthusiasm of clergy and laity alike, bore great fruit. Just as important as the insights gained were the experiences themselves; many participants were so moved that they asked for more opportunities to gather in this synodal way.

The global Synod on Synodality unfolded during the lingering effects of the COVID-19 pandemic, when personal encounters were still limited. Perhaps this made the gatherings even more meaningful. The purpose of the synod was to engage the faithful in reflecting on their faith and discerning how they, as the People of God, might accompany one another on their earthly pilgrimage. The circle method with the Diocese of San Diego proved an ideal way for Catholics to share their experiences and hopes for the Church. Pope Francis, and now Pope Leo, call us not to treat synods as one-time events but to make synodality a way of life.

Today, the Diocese of San Diego is working with parishes to cultivate a synodal culture. Thirty-six parishes, about one-third of the total in the diocese, have been designated as pilot sites for synodality and co-responsibility. These parishes are developing ways for clergy and laity to work together in listening, accompaniment, and shared leadership. Resistance remains in some parishes, but I sense that will diminish as people come to understand what synodality truly is.

Opposition to synodality stems from many sources. Some object on ideological grounds, viewing Pope Francis and Cardinal McElroy as too progressive. Others simply misunderstand the concept. Before 2021, most Catholics had never heard the term, and for many it remains unclear. In truth, synodality simply means journeying together in faith, and loving and supporting one another as Jesus commanded. In everyday parish life, clergy, religious, and laity already accompany one another; synodality invites them to do so more intentionally and collaboratively.

Cardinal McElroy helped author a clear definition of synodality for the global Church: "Synodality is a path of spiritual renewal and structural reform that enables the Church to be more participatory and missionary, so that it can walk with every man and woman, radiating the light of Christ." In essence, synodality is what Christ has always asked the Church to be, a people who welcome all and go forth to proclaim the good news in the Gospel. It means walking together in faith, listening to one another, and supporting each other as one "Body of Christ". Though some opposition remains, I am confident it will fade as more Catholics recognize that synodality is not a novelty, but rather it is the gospel lived out in community.

Synodality and the Criminal Justice System

Early in 2021 I received a call from a law student working with Thomas Donnelly, a judge of the Circuit Court of Cook County, Chicago, to arrange a meeting with the judge. Judge Donnelly is the founding member of the Catholic Criminal Justice Reform Network (CCJRN), affiliated with the Lumen Christi Institute at the University of Chicago. Lumen Christi's mission is "to make the Catholic intellectual tradition a vital part of the secular university and the broader culture." As the oldest continuous intellectual tradition in the world, with its scholarly heritage the Catholic Church provides a deep source of wisdom for the modern world.

Judge Donnelly explained to me that the CCJRN was organizing its inaugural national conference at Georgetown University Law Center in the spring of 2022. From our initial conversation, I quickly sensed that the judge was a man of profound faith. That initial conversation became the beginning of a lasting professional and personal relationship. Judge Donnelly's vision was that the conference provide an opportunity for an encounter between decision-makers in the criminal justice system, including judges, prosecutors, defense attorneys, and law enforcement leaders and those most affected by it: the formerly incarcerated and victims of crime. He proposed that Bishop McElroy and I open the conference with a forty-five-minute dialogue. His goal was to center the dialogue on the voices of the system-impacted. I thought it was a remarkable idea and spoke with Bishop McElroy. The bishop agreed to participate. Although I was honored to be invited, I knew Bishop McElroy would be the main draw for the distinguished audience of scholars, judges, and attorneys.

Robert McElroy is one of the most intellectually gifted people I have ever met. My own faith formation deepened significantly during the six years I worked under his leadership before he was called to Washington, D.C. to become its Cardinal Archbishop. He rarely uses notes when he speaks publicly and often weaves in insights from earlier speakers with ease. A week before the conference, I met with him to discuss key talking points. We agreed to center our dialogue on the gospel vision of justice, particularly drawing from the Parable of the Good Samaritan, and to allow time for questions. The bishop planned to participate only on the first day, as he was scheduled to attend another national conference that week.

The inaugural CCJRN Conference took place in April 2022 at the Georgetown Law Center campus, near the U.S. Capitol. I have attended many conferences over the years, both as a military officer and as a diocesan leader, but this was the first time I served as a keynote speaker on a national stage. Though nervous, I was deeply grateful to share the platform with my bishop. During our conversation, Bishop McElroy reflected on justice as God's design—justice that is relational, merciful, and grounded in love. Using the Good Samaritan as his model, he reminded the participants that at various points in life, we might find ourselves as the victim, the bystander, or the innkeeper, each with an opportunity to respond to suffering with compassion. He also said that he hired me partly because of my lived experience of incarceration—something, I believe, few bishops in the United States would have considered in a candidate for a diocesan leadership role. His public affirmation humbled me deeply.

One of the most powerful aspects of the CCJRN conference was the use of circles for small group dialogue. Each table had seven or eight participants, intentionally mixing judges, prosecutors, law enforcement professionals, academics, nonprofit leaders, and formerly incarcerated persons. Attendance was limited to about one hundred people, creating an atmosphere of intimate, authentic encounter. Judges and prosecutors rarely, if ever, sit in meaningful conversation with the formerly incarcerated, yet here the interactions felt natural and grace-filled.

At the close of the first day, participants walked together from Georgetown Law Center to Holy Rosary Church for Mass, celebrated by Bishop McElroy. My bishop walked side by side with my friends Eddie Blajos and Nadine Goddard—both formerly incarcerated and now leaders in our Kairos House ministry in San Diego. I was profoundly moved to see my bishop, one of the Church's senior leaders, walking and conversing with people who society once discarded. It was a vivid image of the gospel: walking together in charity and faith without judgment or preconditions.

Judge Donnelly's vision for the CCJRN extended beyond that inaugural gathering. He hoped dioceses and organizations across the country would host regional or local conferences using the same circle-based model to bring criminal justice leaders and system-impacted individuals into dialogue. He told me, "True reform begins with the heart—and the only way to change a heart is through personal encounter." His words resonated deeply, and when he asked if I would host a regional event in San Diego, I did not hesitate. In fact, I ended up hosting two.

In spring 2023, my diocesan office co-hosted a dinner and small-group dialogue with the University of San Diego School of Law, intentionally limiting attendance to about one hundred participants. The group included judges, prosecutors, defense attorneys, law students and professors, law enforcement officials, correctional officers, wardens, and more than twenty-five formerly incarcerated men and women; each circle included at least two formerly incarcerated citizens. It was also the first time my own sentencing judge, the Honorable Larry Burns, attended one of my events. The last time we met was in 2013, when he sentenced me to three years in prison. Ten years later, we sat together at the same table.

That evening, Cardinal McElroy, Dean Robert Schapiro of USD Law, and I opened with brief remarks before participants broke into circles for ninety minutes of dialogue. The event drew many prominent local leaders, including San Diego County District Attorney Summer Stephan. At the end of the night, I was asked to take a photo of several formerly incarcerated participants with Roxana Kennedy, the Chief of Police of Chula Vista and president of the San Diego County Police Chiefs' Association. As they posed, the Chief began playfully giving "bunny ears" to some of the participants—a lighthearted, grace-filled moment. In that instant, barriers between law enforcement and the formerly incarcerated disappeared. It was a small but powerful sign of what can happen when people meet one another as brothers and sisters in Christ. I believe the Holy Spirit was working in our circles that evening.

In 2024, the ten dioceses and two archdioceses of California, supported by the California Catholic Conference, decided to host a statewide CCJRN conference titled "Journeying with Hope." The Diocese of San Diego, with my office in the lead, served as the primary host. The one-day event brought together one hundred participants, including thirty-five formerly incarcerated individuals, along with judges, prosecutors, defense attorneys, correctional officers, law enforcement leaders, professors, and nonprofit directors. The dialogues were honest, moving, and at times transformative. My former sentencing judge, now my friend, was one of the panelists. He spoke candidly about rehabilitation and change, calling the experience of meeting so many formerly incarcerated people "cathartic." For me, sharing the room with him again—this time as equals and collaborators—was profoundly healing.

The conference sought to foster sacred encounters among people who are usually adversaries within an impersonal, legalistic system. Judge Donnelly often notes that laws alone cannot change hearts. "When you change hearts," he says, "you create lasting change." The circle process used in these CCJRN gatherings made such transformation possible. It allowed people on opposite sides of the justice system to listen to one another with respect and empathy—living out Christ's command, "Love one another as I have loved you."

At the close of the statewide conference, introducing Judge Burns to another participant, I referred to him as my sentencing judge. He smiled and said, "Just call me Larry—and your friend." I told him I wasn't comfortable using his first name, but I would gladly call him a friend. That exchange captured the essence of what the Holy Spirit can do through mercy and encounter. The journey from judgment to friendship is possible only through love, forgiveness, and grace. I remain deeply grateful that my path has led from anger and shame to healing and peace.

Circle Up

This chapter is titled "Circle Up." Circles—or Council—represent a restorative practice that over the past two decades has gained growing recognition. At its heart, circle work is about participants returning to their shared humanity.

We live in an age of extraordinary technological advancement. Smartphones and social media have become almost essential for participation in modern society. These tools have made it easier than ever to access vast amounts of knowledge and connect across great distances. Yet paradoxically, they have also made it harder to connect on a deep, human level. The same technology that keeps people "in touch" has often left them more isolated.

True human connection, rooted in listening, empathy, and understanding, can be cultivated only through personal encounters. Circles provide space and structure for such meaningful engagement. The Catholic faith is also grounded in encounter: relationship with God through prayer and the sacraments, and relationships with others through dialogue, listening, and physical presence. In circle settings I have engaged in countless beautiful encounters, including sacred moments with incarcerated men, educators, criminal justice leaders, university students, and fellow believers. Circles cannot erase all barriers to honest dialogue, but can significantly reduce them.

Western culture, celebrates the legend of King Arthur and the Knights of the Round Table. The "round table" symbolized equality among the king and his knights, suggesting that hierarchy and power could be set aside in favor of fraternity, respect, and shared purpose. Though a myth, this story offers a timeless lesson: genuine community grows when people meet one another as equals. In many ways, the contemporary practice of dialoguing in a circle embodies that same ancient ideal.

The United States is not alone in facing polarization in political, economic, and religious life. Around the world, access to endless information, much of it unreliable, has fueled division. In the U.S., a sense of moral self-righteousness has taken root across the political spectrum, convincing many that there is only one right way to address problems: my way. This mindset has stifled genuine dialogue and deepened division. The circle method offers a path toward reconnection. It seeks not to change minds but to open hearts—to help people listen across differences and rediscover each other's humanity.

Sadly, polarization has become so entrenched that many no longer believe civil discourse is even possible. Yet our ancestors' wisdom, both spiritual and cultural, remains vital today. Human beings, created for relationship, are called to build understanding through listening, dialogue, and shared journeying. Circle practices foster trust, reduce misunderstanding, and help everyone live the commandment Jesus modeled: love one another as I have loved you.

As a carrier of Council, I am continually reminded of the transformative "power of the circle." This power is not merely human—it is spiritual. Through my Catholic faith, I recognize it as the power of the Holy Spirit working through each person, drawing them into relationship with God and one another. Perfect justice comes through mercy and forgiveness, but listening and understanding establish a foundation for mercy and forgiveness.

Many have experienced the intimate encounter of a circle around a campfire, a family table, or a shared meal.

Relationships grow strong through true listening and appreciation of others' perspectives. At its core, "circle up"—the invitation to gather, listen, and share—is, an invitation to communion. It is the way to reclaim a shared humanity and allow the Spirit to move among all.

Chapter 10

Behold, I Make All Things New

All Things New

Colette and I spent nearly a decade in what felt like an earthly purgatory. Our troubles began in early 2011 when federal agents raided our home and business and informed me that I was the target of a federal investigation. The hardships that followed—trial, incarceration, bankruptcy, and the long aftermath—were relentless. When I was released from prison in 2015, I felt as though I could barely keep my head above water while trying to repair the harm that I had caused my family. We were also in serious financial distress after the collapse of our business and the government seizure of our capital. We endured four separate lawsuits and personal bankruptcy. By late 2019, we had finally settled everything related to my incarceration and our failed business.

A new year and a new decade brought hope. But in 2020, as the world reeled from COVID-19, another crisis struck our family. Our eldest child, Brendan, became gravely ill. It took months to diagnose his mercury poisoning caused by eating excessive amounts of tuna. He lost his ability to think clearly and could not tolerate sunlight. A once confident, strong young man became withdrawn, depressed, and anxious about his future. It took him a full year to recover, supported by an employer who stood by him. He eventually emerged stronger—mentally, emotionally, and spiritually.

These challenges, especially Brendan's illness, pushed me to pray constantly, not for solutions but for spiritual strength and wisdom for myself and my family. I sensed God moving me toward something beyond my immediate circle, calling me to "up my game" and to honor the promises I made to him in prison and on probation. The words from the Book of Revelation spoke directly to me:

> I heard a loud voice from the throne saying, "Behold, God's dwelling is with the human race. He will dwell with them and they will be his people, and God himself will always be with them [as their God]. He will wipe every tear from their eyes, and there shall be no more death or mourning, wailing or pain, [for] the old order has passed away." The one who sat on the throne said, "Behold, I make all things new." Then he said, "Write these words down, for they are trustworthy and true." He said to me, "They are accomplished. I [am] the Alpha and the Omega, the beginning and the end. To the thirsty I will give a gift from the spring of the life-giving water. The victor will inherit these gifts, and I will be his God, and he will be my son. (Rev 21:3-7 NAB)

Through baptism, I am a son of God, and my suffering became a gift that prepared me and my family to serve others in a unique way. In January 2011, I was a very different man than I was nine years later. I was broken by my own decisions that were guided by pride and greed; I was put back together through the love of my family and friends and God's grace. My own brokenness had created a space for God to rebuild me. By cooperating with that grace, I became someone new. God took personal disaster and transformed it, leading me from despair and bitterness toward forgiveness, mercy, justice, and love.

God's Call to the Diaconate

During my time at Florence, a Franciscan priest visited the prison camp once each month. He usually arrived on Wednesday mornings, spent a couple of hours with us, celebrated Mass, and then made his way to the other facilities in the complex. The Catholic inmates felt blessed to have a priest who would come to us consistently. During his visits, we could also receive the Sacrament of Reconciliation (confession).

Through confession I developed a relationship with this kind, understanding Franciscan. About six months before I was scheduled to transfer to home confinement, I went to him for my usual monthly confession. During that conversation, he asked if I had ever considered becoming a deacon in the Catholic Church. I told him that before retiring from the Marine Corps I had once met with my pastor about the possibility, but he advised me to wait. At the time, our blended family, with four young children and the complexities of co-parenting with former spouses, made the prospect unrealistic. Looking back, in 2008 I lacked the spiritual maturity and humility needed to discern a call to ordained ministry.

Nonetheless, in early 2015 the priest suggested I reconsider the diaconate. I chuckled—not disrespectfully, but incredulously. I reminded him that I was currently wearing a green prison uniform and that because of my criminal conviction my future prospects for meaningful employment or ministry were slim. When I left Florence, I had no intention of pursuing his suggestion.

But in 2016 during the trip Colette and I made to the Holy Land everything changed. There, I finally committed to listening to God and following without conditions. For most of my first fifty years, I made all my own plans. I prayed to God and believed in him, but when making major life decisions I rarely sought his counsel, or the counsel of holy men and women. Then, one afternoon overlooking the Sea of Galilee, I felt God calling me in a deeply personal way. Through prayer and tears, I heard him asking me to follow him without conditions and to go wherever he would lead me, even to places I might not want to go.

Living by my own plans had exhausted me. My way had led to incarceration, a failed business, and bankruptcy. On that extraordinary day in June 2016, I finally surrendered, I cried "uncle" to God! With arms outstretched, almost involuntarily, and tears streaming down my face, I gave up my plan and embraced God's. On the same mountain where Jesus gave the Beatitudes, he called me to follow him without conditions. Jesus always gives a choice, and this time I freely chose to follow "The Way"—God's Way.

After my metanoia Colette and I endured several more difficult years, with civil lawsuits and bankruptcy still looming. Yet God provided everything we needed to navigate those challenges. When I finished my doctorate and began working for the Diocese of San Diego, pursuing the diaconate was the last thing on my mind. I had even forgotten my conversation years before with my Franciscan chaplain.

My first job at the diocese involved replacing a retiring deacon who for fifteen years had overseen prison and jail ministry. As a layperson working with the incarcerated and formerly incarcerated, to me the work seemed vocational. In late 2019, just before COVID, Father Eddie Samaniego, SJ, the Director of the Office for the Permanent Diaconate, invited Colette and me to a screening of a film about St. Ignatius of Loyola. We couldn't attend, but the invitation started a dialogue between us about the diaconate.

I still did not want to become a deacon, or at least I didn't want more years of study, training, and formation. When Colette asked why I wanted to be a deacon, I answered honestly: I didn't want to be one, but I had promised God I would follow wherever he led me. We agreed to explore the possibility; we also agreed that if either of us felt it was too much, we would discern out. We approached God's call with caution and some hesitancy, but also with openness, asking God to assist us with discerning his will for both of us.

In the summer of 2020, I began aspirancy, a year of prayer, discernment, and spiritual direction for those considering the diaconate for the Diocese of San Diego. Because Father Eddie is a Jesuit, he required all aspirants to complete the Ignatian Spiritual Exercises. The Exercises are usually performed under the guidance of a spiritual director during a thirty-day silent retreat. They can also be completed over a thirty-week period called the "Nineteenth Annotation," in which a spiritual director guides aspirants in incorporating the exercises into daily life. Colette and I completed the exercises via the Nineteenth Annotation.

We each performed the exercises with our own directors. Colette continued with our pastor, Father Mike Murphy, and I worked with Sister Terri, both of them veterans in Ignatian spirituality. For nearly nine months, we prayed, discerned, and examined our lives, purpose, and vocation. At the end of that period, we were invited into the four-year diaconate candidacy program. The commitment felt enormous, and I struggled with doubts about my worthiness to be a deacon. Father Mike advised me to take it one year at a time, and that is what I did—I simply said yes for one more year.

Candidacy includes four years of Catholic theological study, spiritual direction, faith formation, and pastoral assignments in jails or prisons, hospitals, homeless shelters, and hospice care. In most Catholic dioceses, the wives of deacon candidates are required to participate fully by sharing classes, formation events, and, as much as possible, pastoral assignments. Both husband and wife share in the journey. Colette had been the prime mover in our faith during our marriage leading up to candidacy, and without her complete support and participation I doubt I would have pursued formation. My formation was her formation.

Before entering candidacy, each candidate and his wife must interview with the Vicar for Clergy. At the time, this was John Dolan, now the Bishop of Phoenix. Bishop John had been an auxiliary in San Diego and was my first "bishop boss" when I began working for the diocese. Our interview was relatively relaxed because he knew us well. At the end, he asked Colette if she had any questions. She did.

She asked if it was true that if I were ordained and she died, I could not remarry—I would be required to remain celibate. Bishop John confirmed that canon law requires celibacy for widowed or unmarried permanent deacons. When he asked why this concerned her, she said, "Because he's really needy, and I don't know how he would survive alone." Without hesitation, Bishop John replied, "Yes, he is kind of needy!" We all laughed, and then we were formally invited into candidacy.

Each year of candidacy brought both challenges and graces. In December of our first year, after a short illness and in-home hospice under our care, my father died. Two months later, in February 2022, Colette's mother, Valerie, unexpectedly passed away. In the spring of 2022, my mother fell and shattered her femur in four places, requiring reconstructive surgery, two weeks in the hospital, and two months of rehabilitation in a nursing care facility. These family traumas made us question whether we could continue with formation. I considered stepping away, or at least taking a year off, to care for our family. But God and Colette carried us through that very difficult first year.

My Dad

Richard Joseph Ehnow was, and still is, the most important man in my life. Before I went out on my own, his spiritual leadership in our home and in our faith-community profoundly shaped my own spirituality. He was a man of formidable character, firm convictions, and the strongest faith I have ever encountered. He attended a Jesuit high school, and the Ignatian spirituality influenced him for the rest of his life. He was able to see God's presence in all things and all events. During his memorial Mass I could just picture him beaming as four priests concelebrated, two of them Jesuits.

I was adopted as an infant, and my parents showered me with love, patience, and understanding. I was the "apple of my dad's eye"; we had a very special bond. Like many teenagers, he and I didn't always see eye to eye. At Villanova, I was far from saintly, as my college friends could attest, but I always made it to Sunday evening Mass because I knew my dad would ask if I attended. His influence on matters of faith shaped me, my brother, my mother, and many others as well.

In 2009, at age seventy-eight, my dad underwent hip-replacement surgery. During the operation the surgeon accidentally cut the inferior vena cava, the large vein returning blood from the lower extremities to the heart. After losing several pints of blood it seemed that he was dying. Then a vascular surgeon was summoned to repair the vein, and my dad revived. During those moments, my dad had a near-death experience, and he later told me that he saw himself floating above his body, with St. Monica and St. Cecilia holding his hands. He said it was peaceful and that he was given a choice to stay or return. He chose to return to his family, a decision I imagine was difficult, because he loved God above all others. My dad lived another twelve years, passing away in our home with my mom, my son Brendan, Colette, and me at his bedside.

Why did he return? I won't know for certain until he and I, hopefully, join the saints in heaven. His near-death experience happened about fifteen months before my own struggles began; I surmise he sensed, even if only intuitively, that he would be needed to guide us through that long period of tribulation. He lived long enough to witness my incarceration and release, the resolution of our lawsuits, the end of probation, and Brendan's restored health. During those years I needed him, and he was always there. By the time he died, I was spiritually equipped to lead our family through whatever came next. Only then, I believe, could he let himself finally return to the Lord, whom he longed to see.

Though he never attended college, my dad remains the wisest and most educated man I have known. He never stopped reading, learning, and thinking deeply. Many of our arguments revolved around who was right—and in truth he usually was. He left me many gifts: love, humor, kindness, conviction, and courage.

One thing we rarely discussed, however, was the relationship between justice and mercy. Months after he died, my mom handed me a note in his handwriting that had been tucked into a book. It was a passage from Shakespeare's *Merchant of Venice*, the protagonist Portia's reflection on the "quality of mercy":

> "The quality of mercy is not strain'd.
> It droppeth as the gentle rain from heaven
> Upon the place beneath. It is twice blest:
> It blesseth him that gives and him that takes.
> 'Tis mightiest in the mightiest; it becomes

The thronèd monarch better than his crown.
His sceptre shows the force of temporal power,
The attribute to awe and majesty
Wherein doth sit the dread and fear of kings;
But mercy is above this sceptered sway;
It is enthronèd in the hearts of kings;
It is an attribute to God Himself;
And earthly power doth then show likest God's
When mercy seasons justice" (4.1.190-202)

I believe my dad left this handwritten passage for me. He always told me he didn't care what I did for a living—only that I gave my best. This note was his final reminder that God is both just and merciful, and that justice is perfected through mercy. My dad guided me through my darkest years, helping me recover from incarceration and financial ruin, reminding me that he loved me and, more importantly, that God loves me. I feel my dad's presence daily, especially when I am in intimate conversation seeking God's guidance, and yes, mercy.

God's Graces

Greed and pride led me to incarceration and bankruptcy. God's grace led me out. Many friends have compared our decade of challenges to a modern-day story of Job, and during my diaconate formation, supported every step by Colette, our priorities began to crystallize. The temporal world became less important and less appealing. Both of us felt drawn to live holier, more purposeful lives.

The word *diakonia* means "service." The purpose for which deacons are ordained is to serve the poor, the incarcerated, the widows and orphans, and all those living on the margins. In the early Church the apostles instituted the diaconate for this very purpose, selecting men of character to care for the poor. At the retreat during which we moved from aspirancy to candidacy, the director had us wash one another's feet, just as Christ washed the apostles' feet. This simple act of service demonstrated how pride and ego have no place in the heart of God's servants.

Colette and I spent five years in formation. The three pillars—theological education, spiritual direction and prayer, and pastoral assignments—equipped both of us to serve the Church. Although I was the one who would be ordained, my ministry could not have happened without Colette. Three "yeses" are required for ordination: the yes from God, the yes from the Church through the bishop, and the yes from the candidate's spouse. By early May 2025, I had received all three, and it was time to commit my life to God and his people.

I often told myself I was unworthy. God always answered with the same gentle truth: everyone is unworthy, and he loves all whom he created. On Saturday, May 24, 2025, Bishop Felipe Pulido ordained six of my classmates and me, God's "Magnificent Seven", as permanent deacons for the Catholic Church. As I lay prostrate on the floor of the church, a profound peace and overwhelming sense of love washed over me. I knew the Holy Spirit was fully present. All the struggles of my life had become sources of strength and wisdom, shaping me to serve others with love and courage. God took an ordinary man, allowed extraordinary experiences, and through the love of family and community transformed me into someone new. Deacon Bobby Ehnow was born, another unworthy servant of Christ and his Church.

God is good, all the time!

The Ministry Begins

On the evening of my ordination, Colette and I hosted a family party that included guests who had traveled from out of town. My friend Tony and his wife Amber, came from their home in Riverside County in Southern California, to the ceremony and the party at our house. You may recall from earlier chapters that at the prison camp in Florence Tony and I started the rosary group. He and I also shared the duty of leading the Sunday services for our fellow Catholic inmates. Fortunately, Tony and Amber survived their own encounter with the criminal justice and corrections systems. Tony, a retired law enforcement officer, and I remain friends. I was elated that they were able to attend my ordination and after-ordination family gathering. Later that night, Tony texted me this note:

> "Dear Bobby,
>
> I just wanted to take a moment to say how deeply moved and proud I am to hear about your ordination to the diaconate. That's a profound step—and a powerful witness to what God can do with a willing heart. Your journey hasn't been easy. The road through prison is one many don't come back from with hope, let alone faith. But you didn't just survive—you were transformed. You let God meet you in that place of darkness and shape you into a servant of light. That's not just redemption; that's resurrection.
>
> Being ordained isn't the end of that journey, of course—it's a new beginning. A call to serve, to lift others up, and to be a living testimony that God never gives up on us. You know what grace looks like because you've lived it. And now, you get to share that grace with others who might still be searching for it.

I thank God for your life, your faith, and the path you're walking. You're not just stepping into ministry—you're stepping into a calling that's already been shaped by suffering, redemption, and love.

Congratulations, Deacon Bobby. May God continue to lead you, strengthen you, and use you.

Tony"

I was ordained on a Saturday and the day after I was scheduled to serve as the deacon for the nine o'clock Mass at Sacred Heart Coronado. After proclaiming the gospel, I gave my first homily to the faithful. At that Mass, celebrated by Father Mike Murphy together with our in-residence priest, Monsignor Sheehan, I was installed as a deacon for Sacred Heart. I was humbled with the presence and support of the three fellow parish deacons who were serving alongside me. I was very nervous. This was my first Mass as a deacon, the first time to proclaim the Gospel, and the first time to preach the Word of God. This is what I said to the People of God in Coronado, California:

"Good morning, I am Deacon Bobby Ehnow.

I have been a parishioner at Sacred Heart for twenty-two years. My wife, Colette, and I were married right here in this sanctuary twenty-one years ago. We have a blended family, and we raised our four children, Brendan, Caitlin, Kelly, and Eric, in this parish community. Yesterday, Bishop Felipe Pulido ordained me and six of my classmates as permanent deacons for the Diocese of San Diego for the Catholic Church.

This was a big day for me, my classmates, our wives, our families, and all our loved ones. It is also a big day for Sacred Heart Parish, because I would not be standing right here, today, if not for Father Mike, Father Sheehan, my wife, Colette, the deacons in our parish, and our entire parish faith community.

Our parish is presently blessed with six deacons—Deacon Frank Osgood who is retired, Deacon Bob Griffin, Deacon Kevin Murray, Deacon John Roberts, Deacon Federico Drachenburg, and the newest, baby deacon—me. Our parish is equally blessed with the ladies that are married to our deacons—Ginny Osgood, Mary Griffin, Nancy Murray, Maria Roberts, Claudia Drachenburg, and the baby-deacon's wife, Colette Ehnow.

Many of my family members and friends travelled from all over the country to attend my ordination. Some of my friends and family are here at Mass today as well. I would like to introduce you to three special ladies in my life—Colette—my wife, Elizabeth—my mom; Lucy—my birth-mom (that's right, I am blessed with two moms—both of which are here today).

Many of you, especially those that have known me for more than fifty years are probably thinking right now, "What is Bobby doing up in the sanctuary and proclaiming the Good News to us?" Many may also be thinking, "How the heck did this happen?" My family and many friends can attest that they probably would not have predicted that Bobby, the Bobby that we have known for decades, would someday be ordained in the Catholic Church

As my own life story attests, with God all things are possible! And I am reminded of my place here today by John's words in the Book of Revelation, "Behold I make all things new!" That is exactly what God has been doing for Colette and me for the last five years!

Because of God's grace, and many of you, I decided to cooperate with Jesus in a very personal way, and he led me to the diaconate, and that really means he led me to serve all of you, this parish, our diocese, and most importantly, our Church and God.

Ten years ago, May 24, 2015, literally ten years before I was ordained yesterday, I came back to Sacred Heart for the 9 a.m. Mass after a two-and-a-half-year absence. Ten years ago, I was just released from prison, living in a halfway house, and was granted a four-hour pass because of a letter that Father Mike wrote to the facility administrator asking for permission for me to attend Sunday Mass in my home parish. Ten years ago, I was filled with shame, a lot of doubt in myself and others, and no confidence. I had lost my mojo. I walked up to receive communion thinking the entire parish community was watching me—that was the shame—and before Father Mike gave me the Eucharist, he hugged me and said, "Welcome home!" That was the beginning of Colette's and my own ten-year journey to listen to God and prepare ourselves to serve you!

In this morning's Gospel, Jesus is instructing the Apostles to abide by God's word, and in so doing, they will love God, and the Father will love them. Most importantly, when we love God and abide by his Word then Jesus says "we," meaning God and Son, will dwell within us. Loving God and keeping God's Word results in us sharing in God's own divinity of Father, Son, and Spirit. It is through our baptism, that each of us share in God's divinity and Jesus' three offices as King, Priest, and Prophet. Let me say that one more time, each of us baptized Catholics share in Jesus' divinity as king, priest, and prophet.

God's grace, Jesus' sacrificial death, and the Eucharist all move us closer to God, and allow us to share in God's divinity. We do not become God, but we do become more like God's son, Jesus, through grace, his sacrifice, and our nourishment from the Eucharist.

We receive God's grace initially through our baptism, and then we fortify God's grace each time we celebrate the Eucharist. We are a people of the Eucharist, and the real presence of Jesus resides in each of you. As I stand here right now, I see Jesus manifested in hundreds of faces right before my eyes. The Jesus in you is an awesome spectacle to witness before my very eyes.

For me, this gospel reading is all about saying "Yes" to God. When we abide by God's word, we are saying yes to God! When we love one another, we are saying yes to God! In last week's gospel passage, that is the big ask from Jesus—love one another, and by so doing they will know you are Christians. When we come to Mass to celebrate the Eucharist together, we as a community are saying "Yes" to God!

Nine years ago, Colette and I were on a pilgrimage to the Holy Land. We were staying on Mt. Beatitude on the northern shore of the Sea of Galilee. This is the area where we believe that Jesus preached the Sermon on the Mount and provided us with the Beatitudes. The Beatitudes are the central values for all Christians! I was in the chapel by myself, gazing over the Sea of Galilee, really thinking of the mess that I had made for me and my family—a failed business, a period of incarceration for me, and looming bankruptcy—when God called me.

God was very clear in his call; I was to follow him without conditions, and he would lead me, sometimes to places I do not want to go! I was really tired of leading myself at this point in my life and doing life according to my plan! With my arms outstretched (not my doing) and tears in my eyes, I gave up on my plan, and I committed to follow God's plan. I decided to say "yes" to God without conditions. God calls each of us to do the same—abide in his word, abide in his love! Love one another without conditions!

God gave us the free will to choose his way or our way! For the first fifty years, I did it my way—and at times, it was very hard. In listening to God's voice and following the Way—Jesus' Way—remains the best course for me, Colette, and our family.

Our Church now has a new Pope, Pope Leo XIV, formerly known as Robert Prevost. My life experience is much different than our Holy Father, but we do share one very special experience. We are both graduates of Villanova University. The core values of Villanova are unity, charity, and truth. The Augustinians emboldened me as a young person to live a life of service based on these three values, which is one of the reasons I chose the Marine Corps as a profession for twenty years. Unity, charity, and truth are values that all Christians must share together. They are a part of our spiritual ethos.

I am pledging to you right here today to continue to live these values that I learned more than forty years ago in service to our parish, diocese, and universal Church.

And I have an ask for all of you. First, whenever asked, say yes to God and to others that are in need

> of our love and assistance. That is the essence of the diakonia—the Greek word for service. I and my fellow deacons at Sacred Heart are the sacramental sign of diakonia or service for our Church, and each baptized Catholic is also called to the diakonia, that is to be a servant of God and in service to all God's people—everybody. Through our baptism we share in God's divinity as priest, prophet, and king. Through our baptism we also are called to serve God and others—diakonia.
>
> Question for the day?
>
> How are you called to serve God, his Church, and all you encounter?"

Wounded Warrior

On my last day in prison, my friend Tim walked me to the gate. He was twenty years older, and like me, a retired military officer. During my two years at the prison camp, he was a steady and trusted friend. Tim still had five years left to serve. We looked at each other, fought back tears, and hugged. He held my gaze and said, "You don't ever come back, and you forget all about this place." I promised him I would. I kept the first part of that promise—but I could not keep the second. I cannot forget my prison experience, nor can I forget those who remain incarcerated.

After my release, I vowed never to do anything that might return me to prison. I also vowed to repair the brokenness I had caused my family. Both promises were centered on protecting myself and those I loved. I had no intention of doing anything connected to the criminal justice system. I simply wanted to heal and move forward.

But my metanoia—my conversion—changed everything. My desire to forget and move on was not aligned with God's desire for me. God's grace, and the loving support of many people, led me in a different direction. The wounds from my failures, business collapse, bankruptcy, incarceration, were not meant simply to heal and disappear. They were meant to become sources of compassion and strength, equipping me to love and assist others facing similar pain.

Colette restores the sight of patients going blind from cataracts. She does not need to be blind to heal the blind. In the same way, people can minister effectively to the incarcerated without themselves ever having been incarcerated. Many extraordinary people do exactly that. Yet for me, my lived experience allows me to empathize, understand, and offer comfort in a unique and profound way. I can love without judgment because I continue to cooperate with the graces God has given me. Whenever I am called to help a family with a loved one in jail or to support someone newly released from prison, I begin with prayer and humility—asking God to lead me.

I am not completely healed from my own suffering, and perhaps throughout my life some wounds will remain. Colette and our children carry their own scars from my time in prison. My stepdaughter, Kelly, bears wounds from that period which still linger, and I consider it a commitment and a responsibility to support her healing. Our other children—Eric, Brendan, and Caitlin, also carry scars. Colette and I do not see them as permanently wounded but as continually healing and growing in emotional and spiritual maturity. My wife, children and I are not victims or even survivors of a system that often lacks compassion, and mercy. Rather, we are gifts of God who with wisdom carry wounds, wounds that can love and carry others who face similar challenges.

I have spent much of my life fighting. Some battles were righteous; others were driven by ego, impulse, or sin. I have been a warrior, and I remain one. But now my battling is fueled by the Holy Spirit. I fight for justice and for the dignity of every human person. God does not ask any of us to love passively. He calls us to love actively—with courage and a fighting spirit for justice and righteousness.

We are all pilgrims on a journey. God asks each of us to serve him and one another. God's graces equipped me to serve in a particular way—not in a better way—but simply the way he has prepared for me. I am blessed with a strong, supportive family and countless friends who have guided and loved me through my challenges. I am grateful to you, the reader, for spending time with my story, and I hope you find in it some inspiration that with God's love, you, too, will find that all things are possible.

I close with the words of Jesuit Father Pedro Arrupe:

> Nothing is more practical than finding God, that is, than falling in love in a quite absolute, final way. What you are in love with, what seizes your imagination will affect everything. It will decide what will get you out of bed in the mornings, what you will do with your evenings, how you spend your weekends, what you will read, who you will know, what breaks your heart, and what amazes you with joy and gratitude. Fall in love, stay in love, and it will decide everything.

Thank you for reading my story, and may God continue to bless each one of you.

Epilogue

Timing is everything. For years after my release from prison, friends and family urged me to write this book. I resisted—not because the story was painful, but because it was unfinished. Even when I began drafting during the quiet uncertainty of the COVID pandemic, I knew something essential was still unfolding. What began as a personal story slowly became something larger: a story about accompaniment, about learning how to listen, and about standing alongside others whose wounds ran deeper than my own.

By the time I signed a contract with New City Press in September 2023, I believed I was ready. I promised a completed manuscript within twelve months. When I missed that deadline, I told myself—and others—that formation for ordination had simply taken more time than expected. That explanation was true, but incomplete. The deeper truth is that my life had not yet reached the moment this book required. My ordination had not yet occurred. My ordained ministry had not yet begun. The story could not end until that threshold had been crossed.

A few years ago, I asked my wife, Colette, how she thought I had changed since my release from prison. She answered without hesitation: I was a better husband, a better father, a better listener, and a kinder man. Her words surprised me. I had spent so much time reflecting on what prison took from me that I had not fully acknowledged what it gave me. I never wanted to go to prison, and I still believe our justice system relies far too heavily on incarceration. Yet prison became part of my spiritual formation. It hardened my resolve to live with integrity and softened my heart toward others. Somewhere along the way, I embraced a simple truth: you can never be too kind, and you can never love too much.

A Jesuit friend once told me that every person is called to share their gifts of time, treasure, and talent for the greater glory of God. Before prison, I had confused success with the accumulation of wealth. My gifts were not absent—they were misdirected. Prison became a painful but necessary course correction. It forced me to confront myself honestly and to begin aligning my life with a purpose beyond my own ambition. The journey was messy and often humiliating, but it allowed wisdom, compassion, and love to grow in places where pride once lived.

I write these final words on the Feast of the Epiphany, just after the conclusion of the Jubilee Year of Hope. Pope Francis, whose heart was always close to the imprisoned, designated December 14, 2025, as the Jubilee Day for the Prisoner. That day remains etched in my memory. In the Diocese of San Diego—home to twenty-four jails, prisons, and detention facilities and nearly 24,000 incarcerated people—our bishops and several diocesan priests chose to spend the week celebrating the Eucharist on every state-prison yard within our diocesan boundaries, thirteen yards total. No cameras. No publicity. Just presence.

I accompanied the bishops as an ordained deacon, proclaiming the Gospel and assisting at Mass for men who so often feel forgotten. I watched faces soften, shoulders relax, and eyes fill with tears as the Church showed up

—not in words, but in flesh and blood. In those moments, I understood something I had been circling for years: hope is not an idea. It is an encounter.

Catholics celebrate the sacraments with our incarcerated faithful to offer them love and hope, and to stand in solidarity with them in a shared faith. Jesus taught his followers that justice is perfected with mercy and forgiveness. As Jesus suffered on the cross, he offered hope to the condemned prisoner to his right, who we venerate as St. Dismas, the good thief. St. Dismas asked Jesus, "Remember me, when you come into your kingdom." And Jesus provides him comfort and hope when he replies, "Amen, I say to you, today you will be with me in paradise." Jesus, the Son of God, assures the condemned prisoner that he too has a place in God's Kingdom because of his faith. Today, Jesus offers this same hope and love to all prisoners and their families who believe in him!

Thirteen years ago, I stood before a judge, a federal judge named Larry Burns. Judge Burns has retired as the chief federal judge for the Southern District of Southern California. By Judge Burn's own admission, he was known as a judge that would hand down harsh sentences—often known as a hanging judge. So on May 20th, 2013, in brown prison clothes before many of my friends, most of my family, and several Sacred Heart Parishioners including my pastor, Father Mike, I stood in front of Judge Burns inside a courtroom in downtown San Diego. I had been found guilty of two financial crimes at a trial months before my sentencing hearing, and the federal sentencing guidelines called for eleven and a half to thirteen years in prison. The government prosecutors and federal probation recommended eleven and a half years. We were hoping for half of that time in prison. And then a miracle happened! There were many prayers, including a vigil with Sacred Heart parishioners before the sentencing hearing, many letters in support, and God's own mercy, when Judge Burns provided a sentence that coupled accountability with mercy and the opportunity for me and my family to be restored. The judge sentenced me to three years—a 75 percent reduction in the federal sentencing guidelines. I went to trial, and I lost, and yet, I was provided with mercy that rarely, if ever, occurs in our current criminal justice system. I was provided mercy by the judge through God's own plan, and now I know that I am the recipient of God's justice, perfected through mercy, forgiveness, and unending love!

My gift of mercy comes with great responsibility, and part of that responsibility is to share the story with you and others. We cannot sit on the sidelines when we witness or hear about injustice. We are called to act, whether through prayer and advocacy or whether through direct action. We stand in solidarity with those who through systemic injustice have been treated unfairly or marginalized because they are poor. As the Jesuit, Father Greg Boyle writes, "We go out to the margins because that is where Jesus resides." We do our best to promote justice and care for those on the margins, because without anything that his followers earned or merited, Jesus provided justice for them through his own sacrifice. Christians care for the poor, the newly arriving immigrant regardless of legal status, the prisoner, the widow, the orphans and all those on the margins simply because that is what Jesus would do. Christian faith is guided by what Jesus would do—it is really that simple!

My ordained ministry has begun, and I often feel overwhelmed. The needs are endless, and the work is never finished. I am learning that this, too, is part of the call—to labor without closure, to love without counting the cost, and to trust that God is at work even when my efforts feel small. Each day, I try to say "yes" as often as I can and to cooperate with the grace that continues to shape not only my life, but the lives of those I am privileged to serve.

This chapter of my story has reached its end. But redemption, like grace, does not conclude—it continues to unfold.

Acknowledgements

My spiritual director often reminds me that gratitude is the highest emotion. I am blessed with a loving, supportive family as well as a cadre of many friends.

I am deeply grateful for the support and patience Tom Masters provided me as he edited my book and guided me to complete it. My gratitude extends to New City Press and Focolare Media, particularly Charlie Camosy, Editor of the Magenta Series, that took the chance on me and encouraged me to write this work. Noreen McInnes, another Magenta series author, as well as a friend and colleague, provided frequent encouragement and gentle, positive guidance throughout my writing and editing.

My friend Paul Callan was instrumental in guiding me and holding me accountable to complete each chapter and the entire book. When I had delayed writing the book for an entire year, Charlie suggested that I have a friend or family member help me be accountable with a writing timeline. I immediately thought of Paul, one of my former Commanding Officers in the Marine Corps. Paul did hold me accountable to submit chapters on time, and he did so much more. He guided me to tell my story with the purpose that it provide a greater understanding not only about the criminal justice system, but an understanding of how failure and despair can lead to restoration and at times greater capacity to love and serve. Paul is a remarkable friend, and I do not believe I would have completed this work without his love, guidance, and thoughtfulness on where my writing should focus.

My spiritual director, Sister Terrie Monroe, RSCJ, and my pastor, Father Mike Murphy, are a big part of this story. The many things they have done for me and my family in the last ten years have made this book possible. Their love without judgment, and their spiritual and practical guidance, provided me with the courage and the purpose to tell my story without shame or second thoughts.

I would also like to thank Judge Larry Burns, the judge that sentenced me, and sent me to prison. It sounds crazy to thank the man that sent me to prison, but Judge Burns did hold me accountable for the wrong I did. However, he showed great mercy in his sentencing. Without his mercy, my life would be much different, and I doubt that I would have been able to do the work I have done and continue to do in service to others and God. In the same vein, I would like to thank my criminal defense attorney, Kevin McDermott, not just for his sage counsel and legal defense, but for his friendship and support, particularly his support for Colette and my children while I was in prison.

I am immensely grateful to the leadership team for the Diocese of San Diego for the last ten years, especially Robert Cardinal McElroy, Bishop Michael Pham, Bishop John Dolan, Bishop Ramon Bejarano, Bishop Felipe Pulido, and Marioly Galvan. These Catholic leaders showed great love, patience, and confidence for me and the ministry I lead. I am especially grateful to Cardinal McElroy, who hired me and then allocated the resources for a robust and consequential ministry for the incarcerated men and women throughout the Diocese of San Diego. I am richly blessed by the mentorship and love that my bishops and our Chancellor, Marioly Galvan, provided to me in the last eight years. Nothing good ever happens without strong, committed leadership, and I have been the recipient of such leadership.

Of course, I have to thank my parents, Richard and Elizabeth Ehnow. Anything that I have ever done that resulted in some good can be traced to their love, encouragement and patience. Gratitude goes out to my brother Rich and his wife Patty, who remain steadfast in their love and support of me, Colette, and our kids. My extended family of aunts, uncles, cousins, nieces, and nephews, all never wavered in their love and support while I was in prison and when I returned home.

I have more friends than most men deserve. I certainly want to thank all of my friends that have been and continue to be on this life journey with me. I especially wish to thank my life-long friends that have always stood by me even when I did not want anyone to share my own pain. I have some friends that I know would take a bullet for me and would certainly be sitting alongside me in a jail cell if that's what it took to set things straight. There is no need for last names here, but Craig, John, Brendan, Greg, Hank, Eddie, Mike, Guy, JJ, Matthew, Bruce, Celia, and Trish are among the many that I love and can always count on!

Buddy, Caitie, Kelly, and Eric are my four children that lived the story in this book. They were impacted in a myriad of ways by my incarceration and our financial challenges. They all persevered, and are now all thriving, and serving others as young adults. I am so proud of them, and I am so grateful to have them as my children.

The saying goes that "with every successful man there is a good woman." I am not so sure that I am successful these days, but I do have an immense capacity to love and serve others. It was my parents that instilled the notions of service, faith, and love in me. It is my wife, Colette, that fortifies these notions and all virtues that I possess. Colette is my everything, and she has been so since we first met more than twenty years ago. My friend Paul wrote in the Foreword about my heroic journey, and I will leave it to the reader whether or not you agree that my journey was heroic. However, Colette's journey of love for me and our children is truly heroic. All the cards were stacked against us as we navigated my incarceration, bankruptcy, ongoing child custody issues with her former spouse, and other life challenges. Colette not only led our family during this time, she enhanced her capacity to love me when I felt underserving of such love. She never wavered in her love for me, and still is "all in" with her love and commitment to me and our family. Her love is rooted in God's love for her and all of us. She is quite simply the best person on the planet for me and our children. She's really pretty to boot!

Finally, I would like thank the Triune God that I know loves me. I know that among the billions of creatures that you have created I am not all that special, and yet you have always made me feel that I am the most special, loved person in the universe. Father, thank you for being so gentle, patient and kind. Jesus thank you for dying on your cross, being my friend, and loving me despite all my sins and flaws. Holy Spirit, thank you for being with me, even when I have found myself in some pretty dark moments. You three in one are the best—literally!